AF348659

Orzel

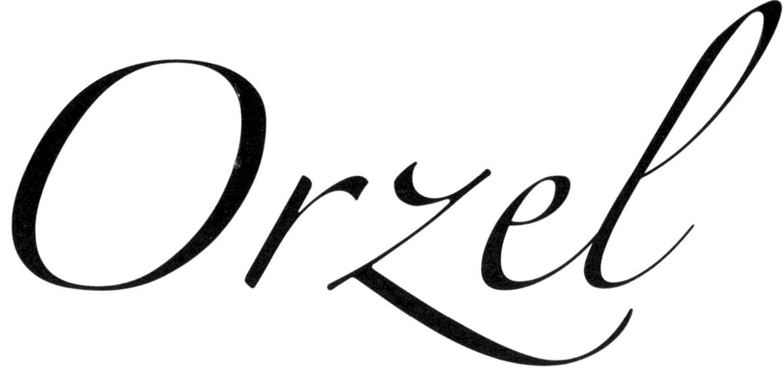

SCOTTSDALE'S LEGENDARY ARABIAN STALLION

TOBI LOPEZ TAYLOR | *Foreword by Stephanie J. Corum*

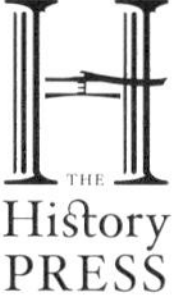

THE
History
PRESS

Published by The History Press
Charleston, SC
www.historypress.net

Copyright © 2016 by Tobi Lopez Taylor
All rights reserved

First published 2016

Manufactured in the United States

ISBN 978.1.62619.962.0

Library of Congress Control Number: 2015953418

Notice: The information in this book is true and complete to the best of our knowledge. It is offered without guarantee on the part of the author or The History Press. The author and The History Press disclaim all liability in connection with the use of this book.

All rights reserved. No part of this book may be reproduced or transmitted in any form whatsoever without prior written permission from the publisher except in the case of brief quotations embodied in critical articles and reviews.

This book is dedicated to my husband, Alan Ferg, and to the stallion LA Orzel, the "best man" at our wedding, a champion reining horse and the namesake of Ed Tweed's imported racing legend.

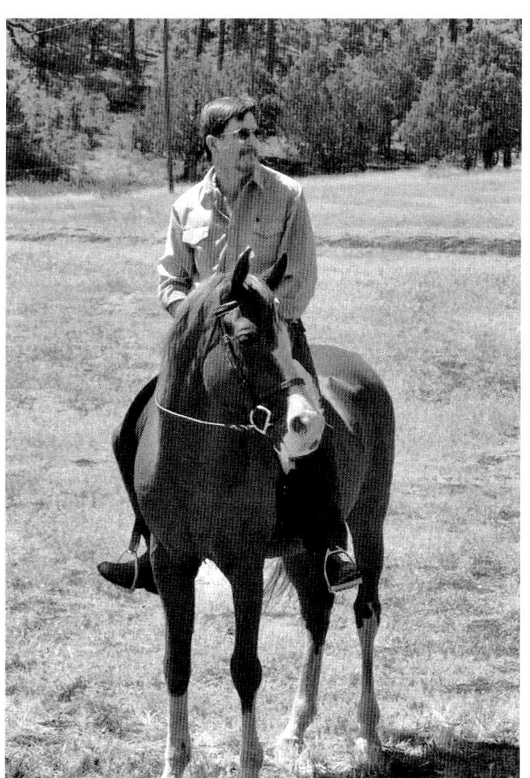

CONTENTS

FOREWORD

An early Arabic saying recounts that "to create the Arab horse, God spoke to the south wind: 'I will create from you a being which will be a happiness to the good and a misfortune to the bad. Happiness shall be on its forehead, bounty on its back and joy in the possessor.'" There is something mystical and majestic about the horse, and no equine exhibits these traits quite like the Arabian. It is a breed steeped in history and legend, the foundation or component of so many other breeds, and it still retains that majesty today. Of particular note is the Polish Arabian. Centuries of breeding have resulted in a well-built horse with a large eye, classic Arabian head and dainty ears. An Arabian aficionado can often pick out a Polish-bred horse based on its looks alone.

The beauty and mystique of the Polish Arabian can be summed up in Orzel's story. His dam, Ofirka, was a young filly in 1939, when Poland's Janow Podlaski Stud evacuated its horses after Germany invaded the country. Ofirka was one of many horses lost, but two years later, she was found on a country farm and returned to Janow. Orzel himself was an impressive specimen, a beautiful chestnut of nearly sixteen hands. He was the perfect stallion to bring fame to Ed Tweed, who purchased and imported the horse in the early years of U.S. Arabian racing.

It is traditional in Poland that a horse must prove itself first on the racetrack before performing in the show ring or the breeding shed. If the horse doesn't succeed as a racehorse, it doesn't pass on its genes. Orzel raced successfully in both Poland and then the United States, where Arabian racing was still in

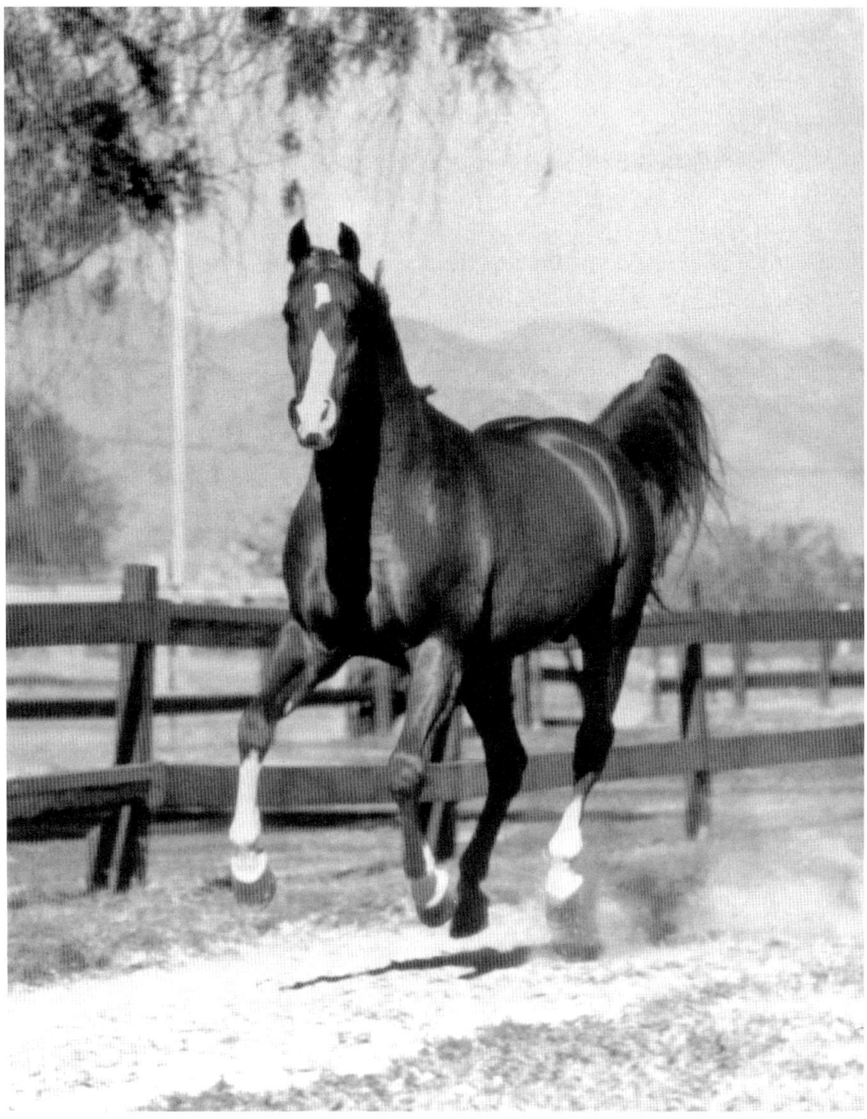

The legendary Orzel epitomized the best in Polish Arabian horse breeding. *Photo by S. Gail Miller, courtesy of Shelley Groom Trevor.*

its infancy. Orzel gave his all in every race. One race that is remembered to this day was a one-and-a-half-mile contest in which Orzel and the equally great Kontiki went head-to-head. They were two heavyweight champions, but on that day, Orzel was the better horse. That contest was both Kontiki's only loss and Orzel's last race.

When his racing career was over, Orzel proved that his athletic conformation also could be appreciated in halter classes, where he was shown to many championships. Then, with Tweed's granddaughter Shelley Groom Trevor, he established the horse/human bond for which Arabians are known. This pair was not only highly successful in the show ring, but they were also true partners. Later, to round out his accomplishments, Orzel proved himself in the breeding shed, establishing his own dynasty. His name still appears prominently in the pedigrees of today's racehorses, albeit further back than it used to be.

The Polish Arabian is strong, proud and loyal—and there is no better example than Orzel. Enjoy his story.

STEPHANIE J. CORUM
Editor, *Arabian Finish Line* magazine

ACKNOWLEDGEMENTS

I would like to thank the following individuals for helping to bring this book to fruition:

Ed Tweed's daughter and granddaughter, Sally Tweed Groom and Shelley Groom Trevor, for their decades of friendship, for their patience in answering so many questions and for allowing me free rein in using documents and photographs from the Brusally archives.

Joni Bockisch, Delinda Ehritz, Susan Daigle-Leach, Alan Ferg and Shelley Groom Trevor for commenting on a draft of the manuscript.

Stephanie J. Corum for agreeing to write the foreword.

Barbara Feighner for her wizardry in preparing the photos for publication.

Andrew Steen for allowing me to reproduce a photo he took of Ofirka, Orzel's dam, and Michael Economopoulos, for allowing me to reproduce a photo of Brusally Orzelost.

Julie Campbell, Gary Clay, the late Gladys Brown Edwards, Chris Evans, Jakub Kasprzak, Richard Loveless, Arlene Magid, Andra Kowalczyk Martens, Roxanne Rogers, John Schiewe and Emilie "Rainbow" Touraine for providing information and expertise that aided in the completion of this book.

Fellow writers Kimberly Gatto and Laraine Herring for their publishing advice.

Melissa Pritchard and the late Elleston Trevor for imparting wise words about writing.

Megan Laddusaw and Jaime Muehl of The History Press for their expertise and their support of this project.

And the residents of Coronado Ranch, particularly Alan, Rosie and Tess, for reasons well known to them.

INTRODUCTION

Once upon a time there was a tall, flashy, charismatic chestnut colt, the well-bred son of two bay parents that was famous for his come-from-behind running style. A sprinter as well as a stayer, he won on dirt tracks and turf courses, beat older horses, carried weight up to 142 pounds, defeated his archrival, competed in two countries—and was associated in the public eye with a lovely blond woman.

A fan of Thoroughbred racing might assume this description refers to Secretariat, the 1973 Triple Crown winner, but in fact it does not. Years before Secretariat came along, Arabian horse racing fans reveled in the exploits of their own chestnut champion: Orzel.

This big red colt, born in 1963 at Poland's Janow Podlaski State Stud, was the last foal of Ofirka, a mare that had barely survived the German occupation of Poland in 1939 and, years later, was marched through Dresden, Germany, hours after the first firebombing had taken place. Orzel's sire, Pietuszok, was born in the USSR and exported to Poland in 1958, where he became a noted sire of stakes winners and record holders.

Orzel's first year of racing took place in Warsaw, where the slowly maturing colt faced off against the best runners of his era, winning two races and never finishing out of the money in his six valid starts. Ranked second on the list of money earners for 1966, the colt was favored to win the next year's Polish Derby.

It was about this time that Ed Tweed, a longtime Arabian breeder, became interested in Arabian racing, and he wanted to win. Knowing that top racing

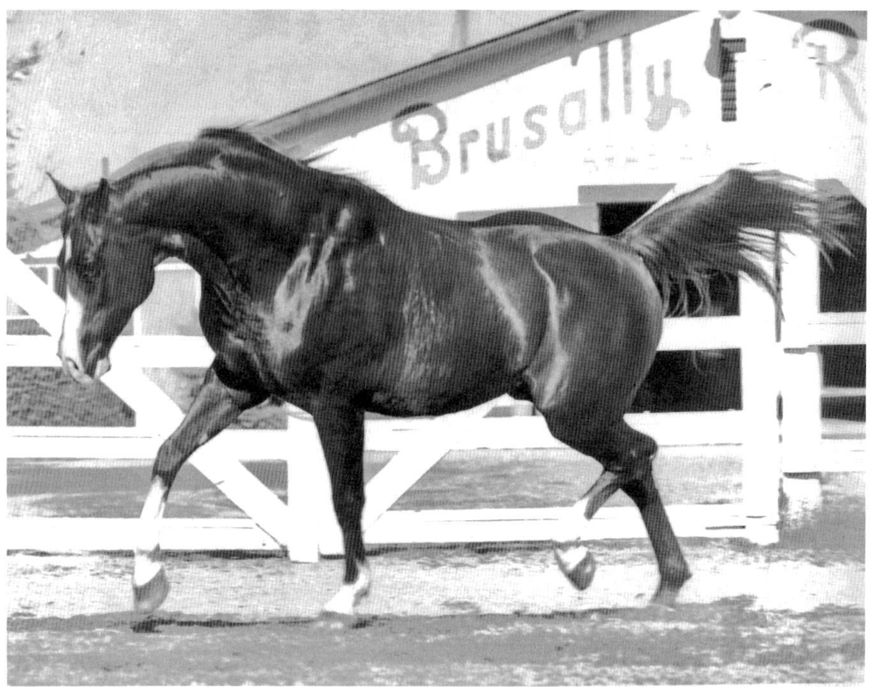

Some have called Orzel the "Secretariat of Arabian racing." Orzel's Triple Crown consisted of his championships in racing, halter and performance. *Photo by S. Gail Miller, courtesy of Shelley Groom Trevor.*

stock came from Poland, he dispatched his trainer, Denis Scully, to buy Orzel. In the spring of 1967, Orzel—whose name means "eagle"—was flown by jet to New York, where he was then shipped to Tweed's Brusally Ranch in Scottsdale, Arizona.

During the 1967–68 racing season, Orzel participated in the first Arabian parimutuel races to be held in the United States, in Lafayette, Louisiana, and Phoenix, Arizona. Despite frequent changes of riders, an intermittent training schedule and steady increases by the handicappers in the weight he carried, Orzel triumphed in four of his five parimutuel starts. In his final race, he emerged victorious over the previously unbeaten Kontiki, a legend in his own right. Orzel was named the first Arabian U.S. National Champion Racehorse, and he retired from racing in the spring of 1968.

Unlike many well-bred Thoroughbred colts, however, Orzel's career didn't end when he stepped off the racetrack. Tweed wanted his champion racehorse to become a champion show horse, so Orzel transitioned from being a racing machine to learning to stand still at the end of a lead line.

Over the next few years, he was named champion stallion at numerous shows, including the Scottsdale Arabian Horse Show, and capped off this phase of his career by being named U.S. and Canadian Top Ten Stallion.

After success as a racehorse and halter champion, Orzel was trained to be a lady's mount—the lady in question being Tweed's young granddaughter, Shelley Groom Trevor, a lovely blond rider who represented Brusally Ranch in the show ring. Theirs was a meeting of minds and souls, a kind of alchemy that was apparent to many spectators, including Walter Farley, author of *The Black Stallion*, who became an admirer of the flame-red horse and his petite rider. Soon, Trevor and Orzel were garnering championships at horse shows across the country. Orzel was named U.S. National Top Ten English Pleasure and won the first U.S. National Champion Ladies' Sidesaddle class. But Trevor valued their quiet times together just as much as their time in the limelight, whether it was a trail ride through the Arizona desert or a few laps around the ranch's half-mile track.

In 1976, Orzel won his last major championship, and Trevor's ride on the big red stallion—which she still calls her "horse of a lifetime"—was at an end. Orzel went on to be the sire of ninety-eight foals, many of them champions, and the grandsire of one thousand more. Today, thirty-odd years after his death, Orzel's bloodlines are found worldwide, in horses participating at the highest levels of Arabian racing, endurance riding, dressage, reining and other disciplines. They are in demand for their extraordinary athletic ability and appreciated for their trainability, intelligence and demeanor.

Although Orzel's achievements have, through the decades, become legendary, in truth, his record needs no burnishing; the facts speak for themselves. In the pages that follow, those who are familiar with Orzel's story will have the opportunity to relive it, while readers who are encountering him for the first time will, I hope, gain an understanding of, and appreciation for, this great Arabian stallion, which one observer called—rightly—"a horse ahead of his time."[1]

Chapter 1

THE WILD EAST SHOW

Like many large land mammals, horses were first viewed by humans as a source of food. Then, "somebody figured out, between 10,000 and 6,000 years ago, that capturing them, breeding them, and riding them might actually be a better idea."[2] As horses were domesticated, and later bred for different characteristics, they began to play important roles in human history—in exploration, transportation, farming and warfare and as symbols of economic status, authority and spirituality.

Contrary to its name, the breed known today as the Arabian horse did not originate on the Arabian Peninsula; instead, it came from "those areas of southern Turkey, northern Iraq, Syria and Jordan that contain the villages or summer encampments of nomadic Bedouin tribes."[3] Scholars differ in their estimates of just when the Arabian horse emerged as a distinct breed; for example, Cynthia Culbertson suggests that these equines "exhibited homogenous characteristics" by AD 570, whereas Deb Bennett posits that, between AD 700 and 1200, the breed known as the Arabian horse was created "by a few Bedouin families who acquired bloodstock through trade, as gifts and possibly by capture from the wild."[4]

Subsisting in an extremely harsh desert climate, where they engaged regularly in intertribal warfare on horseback, Bedouins bred Arabians to be fast, hardy, brave, intelligent and sound. These horses were "accustomed to being deprived of plentiful water supplies and of regular grazing for months at a time, and could survive on such meager fare as *saman* [chopped hay and straw], or dry barley, locusts, [and] dates."[5] For the most part, Bedouins preferred to ride mares, as they were considered to be quieter than stallions, as well as less affected by heat, hunger or thirst.[6] Furthermore, a mare was often kept in the tent of her owner. As one writer noted in 1894, "The mare is the darling of the sheik, the pet of the family. She is treated as a child, far better really than the children…The Bedouin cannot be induced to sell a mare. It is in her that he takes chief pride…it is to her that he trusts his life."[7]

Purity of bloodlines was of paramount importance to the Bedouins, who could recite their horses' pedigrees for several generations. Indeed, the Arabian is among the oldest horse breeds in the world, and when bred to horses of other breeds, it has long been known for its ability to improve them. To cite a few examples, the Thoroughbred racehorse descends from a number of Arabian, Barb and Turkoman stallions—collectively known as "Eastern" or "Oriental" horses because these breeds came from the Middle East and North Africa—imported to England beginning in the mid-1600s and then bred to native British mares. The Shagya-Arabian, a breed that originated at Hungary's Babolna Stud (founded in 1789), resulted from mating Arabians with Thoroughbred, Hungarian and Spanish mares; it carries a very high percentage of Arabian blood and is almost indistinguishable from the purebred Arabian aside from its greater height and body mass.[8] And the popular warmblood breed known as the Trakehner, often seen in show jumping, dressage and eventing competitions, was established in 1732 in what is now Poland. The breed began as an amalgam of Eastern, Thoroughbred and native horses and to this day receives regular infusions of Arabian, Shagya-Arabian and Thoroughbred bloodlines.[9]

While early European travelers to the Middle East and Near East were impressed by Arabians' beauty and endurance, the Bedouins themselves had not bred these horses particularly for their looks. As Emir Abd-el-Kader, an Algerian military and religious leader, wrote to French general Melchior Joseph Eugene Daumas in the 1850s, "According to the sayings of our forebears, we should judge the horse more by his character [moral attributes] than by his appearance. By outward indication one can judge the breeding. From character alone, you will have confirmation of the extreme care which is taken in breeding and of the vigilance which has been exercised to adamantly prohibit misalliances."[10]

Bedouins were understandably reluctant to part with their prized horses, particularly their fillies and mares. They kept only the best colts as future breeding stallions and sold the lesser-quality ones to the inhabitants or horse dealers of the towns they visited.[11] As scholar Donna Landry has noted, Arabian and other Eastern horses were acquired by Europeans in the

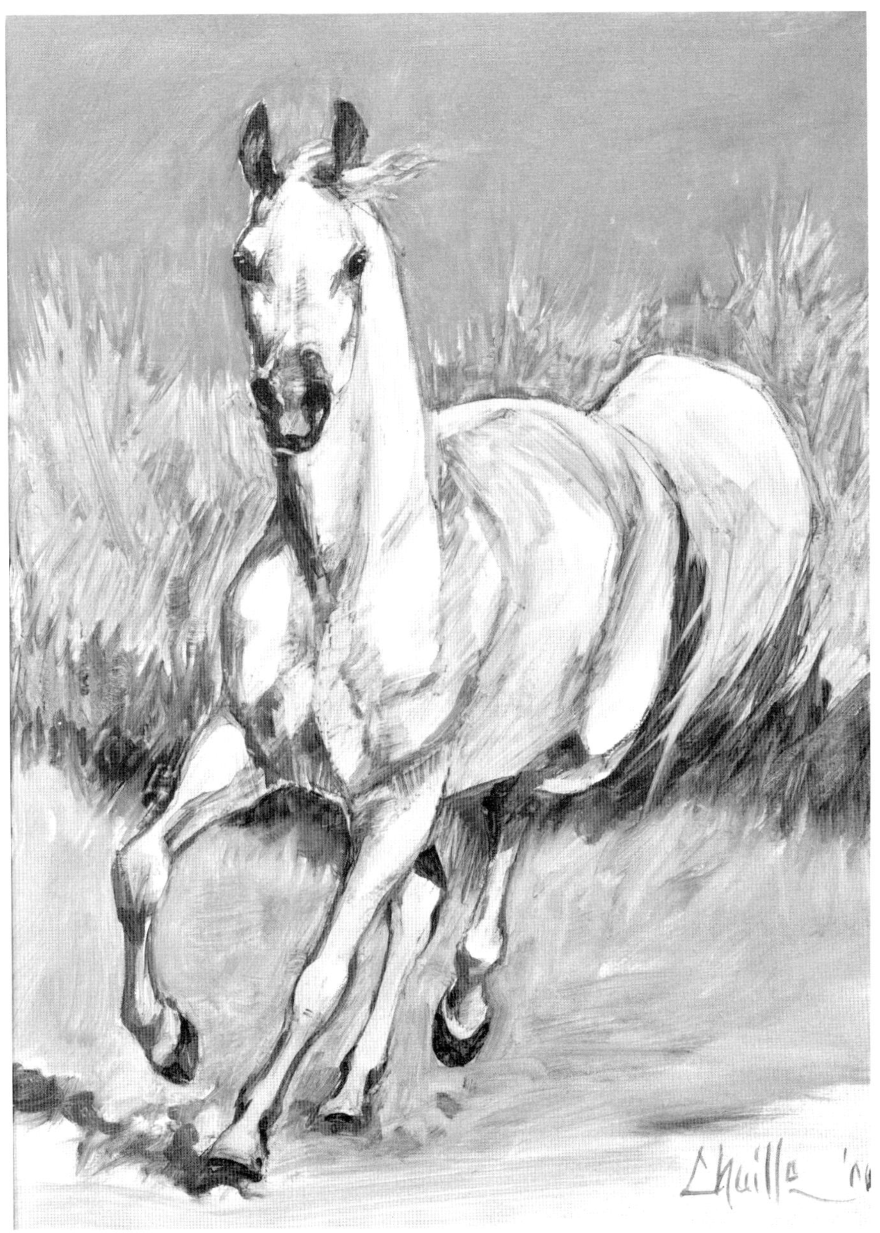

Arabian horses have long been prized for their endurance, character and beauty. Shown here is a painting of an Arabian mare by Chaille (Shelley Groom Trevor). *Courtesy of the author.*

seventeenth and eighteenth centuries as prizes of war, through trade or as diplomatic gifts. She also points out that of the more than two hundred Eastern horses imported to England between 1650 and 1750, "there developed a tendency to name these horses 'Arabians' [even if they were not,] rather than 'Turks' or 'Barbs.'" This was "grounded in an aristocratic preference for a more purely Arabian lineage, emphasizing the supposed purity of Bedouin horse-breeding practices."[12]

When Eastern horses began to be exported to the New World in the 1700s, this preference for the blanket term "Arabian" seemingly traveled with them. For example, John Ferdinand Dalziel Smyth, a British soldier, wrote in 1772 that Thoroughbred horses in Virginia descended from various stallions, including "the Cullen Arabian, the Cumberland Arabian, and a horse from Arabia named Bellsize."[13] Arabian horse expert Gladys Brown Edwards believed that most of the early imports were "of doubtful authenticity, but there were some nevertheless which may have been purebred [Arabians]." Both Edwards and another Arabian horse researcher, George H. Conn, credit Thoroughbred breeder Alexander Keene Richards, of Kentucky, as the first importer of what Edwards called "undeniable Arabians" in 1853 and 1856.[14]

However, almost forty years passed before a large portion of the American public got its first look at true Arabian horses, when a number of them were on display at the World's Columbian Exposition (also known as the Chicago World's Fair). Celebrating the 400th anniversary of Christopher Columbus's arrival in the New World, the exposition was held from May to October 1893. The fairgrounds, which covered more than six hundred acres, featured displays from forty-six countries and were visited by an estimated twenty-seven million people—at a time when the total United States population was about sixty-seven million.[15]

By decree of Sultan Abdul Hamid II, the Ottoman Empire's primary contribution to the fair was a reproduction of the Ahmet II Fountain, an ornate square building with several domes that was originally built in the early 1700s in front of Topkapi Palace in Istanbul, Turkey. Other buildings were constructed for the occasion; objects on display included antiquities, agricultural products, textiles and related items, minerals, electrical appliances, munitions of war and other objects.[16]

The fair also featured an area known as the Midway Plaisance, characterized as a "magnificent sideshow" of exotica.[17] There, the concessions—such as a Ferris wheel, the Street of Cairo, an Irish castle, a Viennese beer garden and a Japanese temple—were mounted by businessmen from throughout the world. One concession from the Ottoman Empire included a Turkish village, with its Street of Constantinople, as well as a 60-foot mosque with a 135-foot minaret, a refreshment pavilion serving fruit drinks and sorbets, a Persian tent featuring a silver throne, copies of Cleopatra's Needle and a Greek monument, cottages, a theater and a shopping bazaar. Affiliated with the Turkish village was a Bedouin encampment underwritten by a consortium known as the Hamidie Hippodrome Society, named in honor of Abdul Hamid II, who, decades earlier, had given President Ulysses S. Grant two Arabian stallions, Leopard and Linden Tree.[18]

For the fair, the Hamidie Hippodrome Society imported forty purebred Arabian horses, as well as twelve camels, seven donkeys and three sheep to re-create a Bedouin camp and put on mounted performances, known variously as the Ottoman Hippodrome and the Wild East Show.[19] Among those who came to see the spectacle were Henry Babson, Peter Bradley, Randolph Huntington, J.A.P. Ramsdell, Henry K. Bush-Brown and Homer Davenport, all of whom either already were, or later became, breeders of Arabian horses. (Years later, Bush-Brown and Davenport would be among the founding members of the Arabian Horse Club of America.) Davenport, who in 1893 was an artist on the staff of the *Chicago Daily Herald*, was

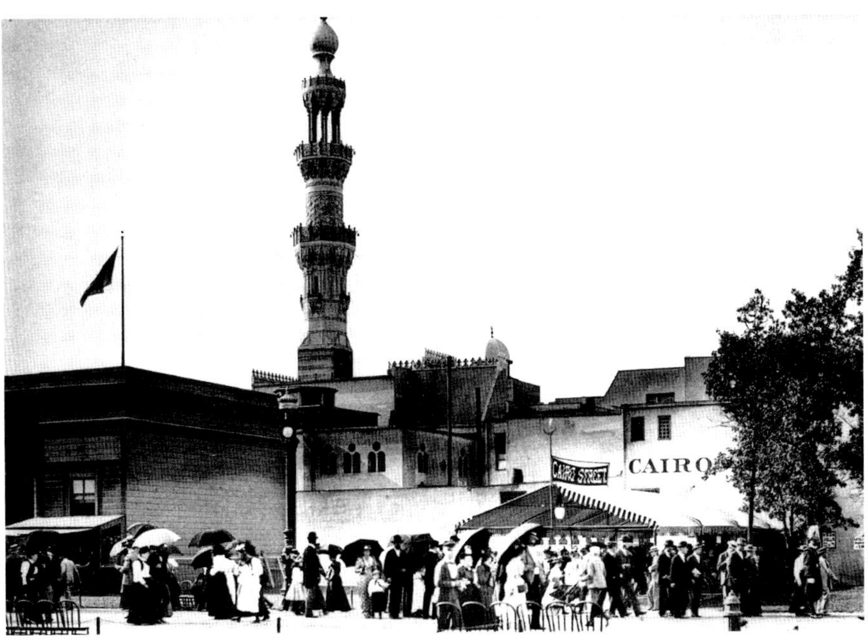

The Street of Cairo was a popular attraction at the 1893 World's Columbian Exposition in Chicago. *Courtesy of Wikimedia Commons.*

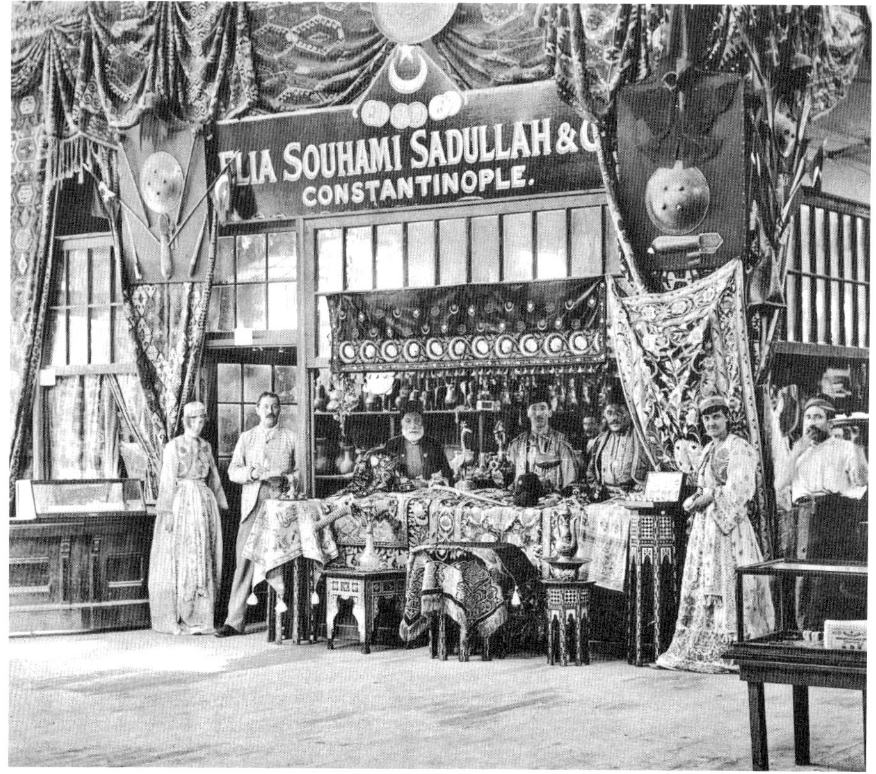

A Turkish bazaar at Chicago's 1893 World's Columbian Exposition featured wares that were exotic to most American visitors. *Courtesy of Wikimedia Commons.*

accompanying one of the newspaper's reporters when they encountered some of the Hamidie Society members riding horses on State Street, near the fair. Davenport later wrote:

> *Though never having before seen a horse with a speck of Arab blood in his veins, I knew that these were Arab horses…I followed those horses—up one street and down another, until they finally arrived back at their headquarters. Here, with about eight thousand small boys, I was stopped at the outside gate while the horses, with big sparkling eyes and gracefully carried tails, pranced in.*[20]

Another contemporary account reported that

> *the character of the entertainment was something on the order of Mr. Cody's* [Wild West] *show, consisting principally of daring feats of*

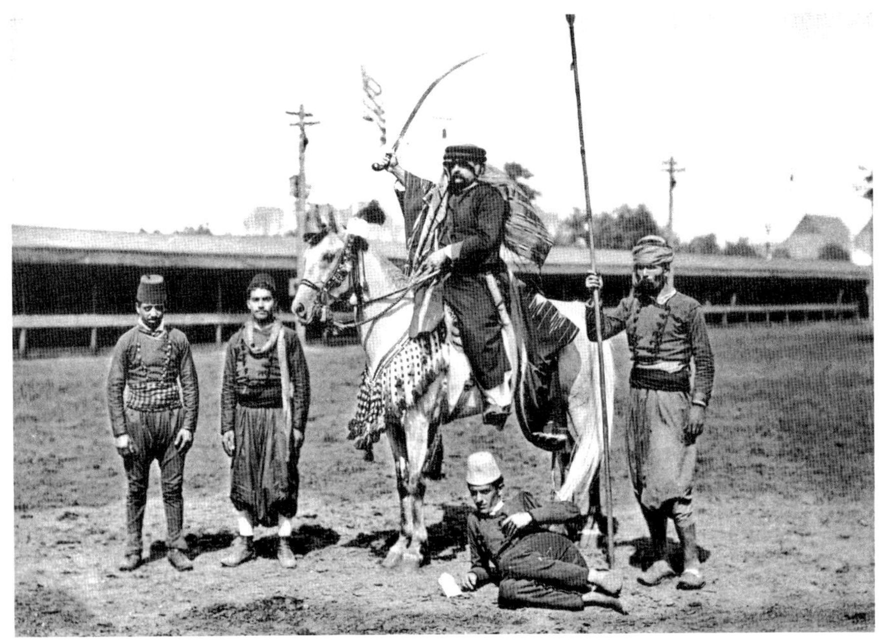

Members of the Wild East Show at the 1893 World's Columbian Exposition in Chicago. *Courtesy of Wikimedia Commons.*

> *astonishing horsemanship, etc. given by a company of Bedouin Arabs. The novelty of the performance made it interesting. The group…in feats of equestrianism held the audience almost spell-bound. Dashing like the wind across the open space reserved for exhibition purposes, these wild sons of the desert seemed almost like demons in their impetuous and fierce display of skill.*[21]

Although the Wild East Show proved to be an inspiration for Americans to buy and breed Arabian horses, the show itself was a financial disaster for its backers. A number of horses died in a fire, unexpected expenses and fees of all kinds mounted quickly and, despite the show's popularity, the Hamidie Hippodrome Society went bankrupt. While the hundreds of performers and other people involved with the Wild East Show were sent back home, their remaining horses stayed behind in Chicago, where twenty-eight of them were sold at auction.[22]

On July 20, 1893, at the height of the World's Columbian Exposition and the Wild East Show, Chicago businessman Fred Tweed and his wife, Emma, celebrated the arrival of their third son. Christened Edwin James

Tweed, he would become one of the best-known Arabian horse breeders of his generation, a founder of the Scottsdale Arabian Horse Show and the importer of many Polish and Russian Arabians, including the celebrated racehorse, show horse and sire Orzel.[23]

Chapter 2

A SORT OF MAGIC

Edwin James "Ed" Tweed was the third of three boys born to Frederick H. "Fred" Tweed and his wife, Emeline Goodrich Tweed, known as Emma. Fred was the son of an Irish immigrant, John Tweed, and Jane Montgomery Tweed; Emma's parents were Theodore Goodrich and Grace Mills Goodrich.

Although both Fred and Emma Tweed were native New Yorkers, they actually met in Portage, Wisconsin, a small town about two hundred miles northwest of Chicago. According to a 1937 article in the *Wisconsin State Journal*, Fred started out as an interior decorator on the East Coast and moved to Chicago to work for a decorating firm there.

> *He was sent to Portage to decorate a new church. While working there he met THE young lady* [Emma] *and when the church was finished he quit his job and settled in Portage, where he was married. He took up sign painting and then began to make signs. His business grew rapidly but when because of freight rates on glass he could not compete with others, he removed to Chicago, where he developed the largest glass sign plant in the world.*[24]

It was to Portage that Emma Tweed returned to deliver each of her three sons: Ralph in 1888, Carleton in 1891 and Edwin in 1893. Although Portage was, and remains, a small community, it is associated with a number of important people, including naturalist John Muir, environmentalist Aldo

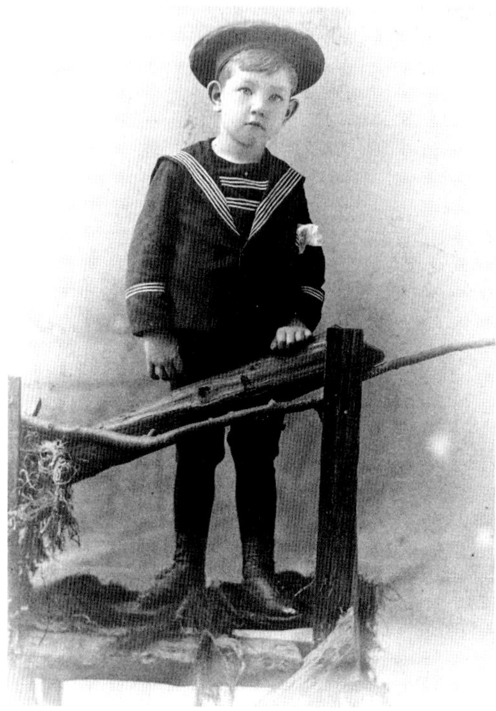

A young Ed Tweed. *Courtesy of Shelley Groom Trevor.*

Leopold, historian Frederick Jackson Turner and Zona Gale, the first woman to win a Pulitzer Prize in drama.

In 1905, Fred Tweed became just the thirty-ninth member of the fledgling Rotary Club (now Rotary International), a service organization that had been established only the year before by attorney Paul Harris and three other businessmen in Chicago. Within a few months of joining Rotary, Fred invited Don Carter, his patent attorney, to become a member. When Carter read the brochure outlining the organization's narrow mission—to promote its members' business interests, good fellowship and "other desiderata ordinarily incident to social clubs"—he was unimpressed, noting that "such a club has great possibilities if it could do something of benefit to people besides its own members. I believe it should do civic service of some kind." Tweed encouraged Carter to join the organization and write a draft amendment to the mission statement. Carter's addition was adopted in 1906, and Rotary's focus shifted to community service. Today, Carter is known as the organization's Father of Community Service.[25]

In 1909, Harris sent Fred to New York City to form the first Rotary Club there. Later, Harris wrote:

Freddie is big, hale and hearty, and possesses a magnetic personality; his manifest geniality impresses even the passing stranger. Men stop on the street, take a second look at him, smile broadly and pass on. Waiters in restaurants, shop-keepers, news boys give him special service and attention. Their service is spontaneous. Wherever he goes he gets the best of everything. What does he give in return? Nothing, that he is conscious of. He is just him self [sic]—genial, kindly old Freddie, and he looks the part. He never learned how to be a gentleman; he didn't need to; he was born that way.[26]

Fred Tweed's sons all inherited his work ethic and drive. The eldest, Ralph (1888–1974), became the president of the Austin News Agency, a newspaper distributor, in the Chicago area. Carleton (1891–1970) trained as an engineer and later became a philanthropist, along with his wife; their Lady Suzanna P. and Carleton Tweed Charitable Foundation, headquartered in Coral Gables, Florida, continues their work.[27] And Ed, who was perhaps the most like his father, had Fred's artistic ability, extroverted personality, business acumen and devotion to civic duties—including membership in his father's beloved Rotary Club.

Like the other Tweed boys, Ed was brought up in Chicago, where he attended the Lewis Institute, which at one time was the first junior college in the United States and is now part of the Illinois Institute of Technology. Upon graduation, he entered the field of bank engineering. Ed recalled later that "those were the days of big, ornate banks, and we designed everything from the elaborate façade to the drawers and hinges in the tellers' cages and the complex vault system."[28] His first jobs out of school took him to various parts of the country, and in 1920, he settled in Kansas City, Missouri, with his young wife, Ruth (née Phillips); daughter, Marjorie (known as Sally); and son Bruce. Five years later, Ed and a partner, Charles A. Lane, established Lane & Tweed, Bank Engineers, about which it was said in 1931:

> [The firm] *has specialized along lines of bank protection and has gone very thoroughly into the matter of bank security against robbery, a subject of tremendous importance to banks and to depositors. In fact, the entire field of bank design, equipment and protection is well covered by the firm, which has taken for its creed 100 percent satisfaction for its clients.*[29]

Understandably, the field of bank design was a casualty of the Great Depression, as existing banks failed and new ones were rendered unnecessary. Ed recalled that he "worked three years on a bank that failed as soon as it opened…that broke us."[30] The Tweeds relocated to Independence, Missouri, where Ed rented part of a bank that he had designed, converting it into the Moderne Sweet Shoppe and Tea Room, whose regular customers included Harry S Truman, then a county judge.

Some years earlier, Ed's father had sold his sign business and had become "interested in the manufacture of brass valves, taking over the management

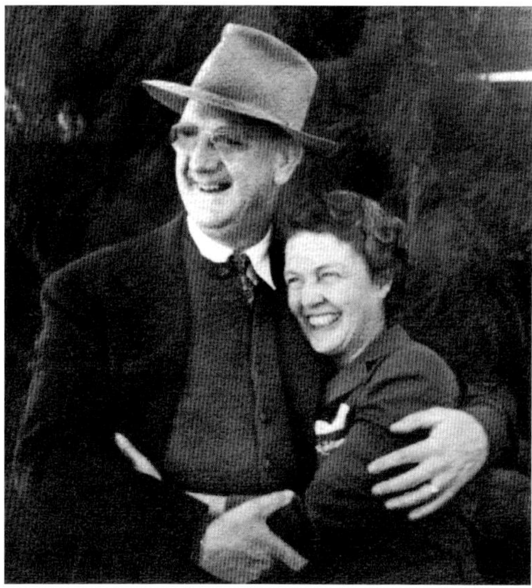

Ed and Ruth Tweed in the 1940s. *Courtesy of Shelley Groom Trevor.*

of a comparatively small plant in Chicago and building it up to one of the largest in the country."[31] By 1935, this firm, the Dole Refrigerating Company, was faltering, and Fred asked his youngest son to move back home to help close it down. Instead, within a few years, Ed turned the company's fortunes around, becoming its president and principal stockholder.[32]

By 1941, Ed and Ruth's much-improved financial situation allowed them to realize one of Ed's lifelong dreams: to have a home in the country and breed livestock, including horses. Ed set his sights on residing in the village of Lake Forest, Illinois, north of Chicago. "Situated along the western edge of Lake Michigan's bluffs and beside deep ravines," Lake Forest had been home since the 1850s to "hundreds of elegant country estates [that] house[ed] the families of Chicago's commercial, professional, and cultural leadership"—including members of the McCormick and Wrigley families, whom the Tweeds would later come to know well as fellow Arabian breeders.[33] When the Tweeds began looking for acreage in Lake Forest, the area was undergoing a transformation owing to the Great Depression and other factors, meaning that "some of the grand manor houses faced partial abandonment or demolition, and landscaped estate grounds and gardens were truncated or subdivided when owners could no longer maintain them intact."[34] Ed and Ruth were able to purchase land from the family of meatpacker of Gustav Swift, and Ed built a house, horse stable and cattle barn in the Old English style. (The house, on Glenwood Road, is still standing.) The Tweeds' new home was christened Brusally, which combined the names of the Tweeds' son and daughter, Bruce and Sally. They acquired some riding horses, as well as cattle and pigs.

Although the Tweeds greatly enjoyed their pastoral lifestyle in Lake Forest, they soon began to winter in Arizona. A 1943 article in the *Chicago Tribune* mentioned that Ed and Ruth stayed at Tucson's El Conquistador

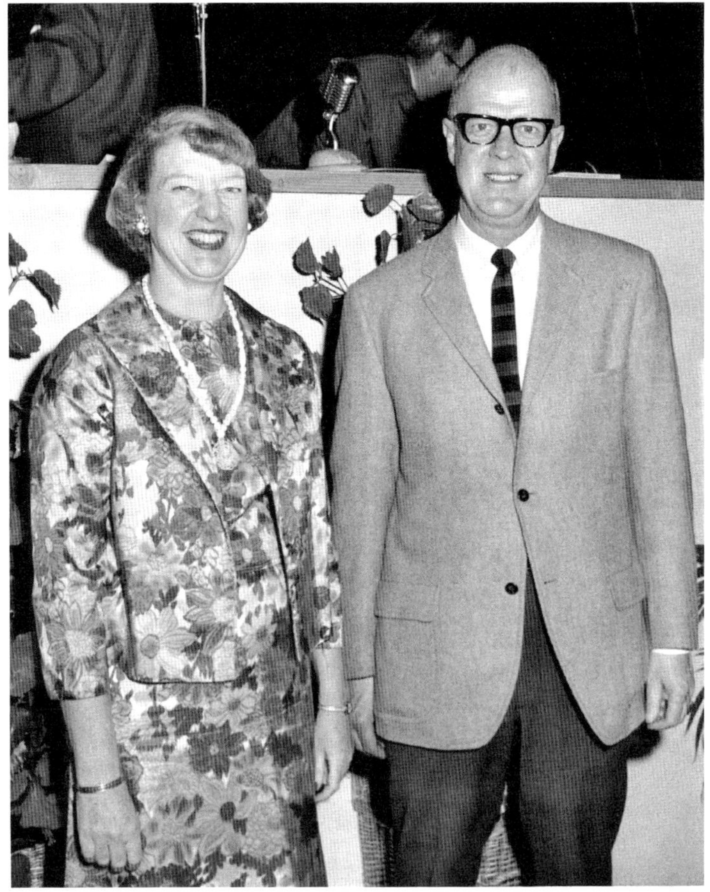

Sally Tweed Groom and her brother, Bruce Tweed, for whom Brusally Ranch was named. *Courtesy of Shelley Groom Trevor.*

Inn.[35] Another article, from 1946, noted that "chilly breezes from Lake Michigan already are sending many Chicagoans scurrying toward sunnier climates…As in other seasons, the Camelback Inn [near Phoenix, Arizona], which will open Friday, will be a popular vacation center for a large colony of Chicagoans"—including Ed and Ruth Tweed, who were listed among those who would be present at the inn's season opening.[36]

During one trip to Scottsdale, Arizona, in the 1940s, Ed made the acquaintance of Merle B. Cheney, a realtor, Arabian breeder and retired chemist who was credited with "developing the oxygen tent and the first filter to enable people to stop smoking."[37] At that time, Arabian horses were still fairly rare in the United States, with only about three thousand registered by the Arabian Horse Registry of America between its inception in 1908 and 1945. It was at Cheney's ranch in Scottsdale that Tweed initially encountered Arabian horses in the flesh. In fact, the first two Arabians he purchased were acquired from Cheney: the gelding Malachi and his sister, the mare Nineveh, bred by Cheney from stock he had acquired from cereal manufacturer and noted breeder W.K. Kellogg. Tweed, with his artist's eye, was enchanted by the look and demeanor of Cheney's equines, so different from the riding horses Ed had purchased in Illinois: "They were sort of magic, [combining] a classic purity in conformation and movement with a gentle and affectionate disposition."[38] Just as Homer Davenport's life changed the instant he encountered the Arabians of the Hamidie Hippodrome Society in 1893, Ed now felt compelled to collect and breed these horses.

Interestingly, Tweed wasn't the only Chicagoan who became smitten with Arabians and bought a home in Arizona. Chewing gum manufacturer and Chicago Cubs owner Philip K. Wrigley and his wife, Helen, began breeding Arabians in the 1930s and passed through Arizona each winter, bringing their horses with them. Each year, they stayed at the family's Wrigley Mansion, adjacent to their Arizona Biltmore Hotel in Phoenix, before embarking for their ranch on Catalina Island, off the coast of California. Influential breeder Ruth "Bazy" McCormick Miller (later Tankersley), daughter of Senator Joseph Medill McCormick and Congresswoman Ruth Hanna McCormick, established her Al-Marah Arabians in Tucson, Arizona, in 1941 and went on to breed more than 2,800 Arabians.[39] In 1947, socialite Anne McCormick and her husband, Fowler—a distant cousin of Bazy Tankersley and a grandson of both Cyrus McCormick, inventor of the McCormick Reaper, and John D. Rockefeller, Standard Oil cofounder and philanthropist—bought land in Scottsdale and purchased an Arabian stallion, Mustafa, soon thereafter. Anne bred a number of champions before her death in 1969.[40]

What brought so many people to Arizona, and particularly the Phoenix area, in the 1940s? Phillip and Mary VanderMeer noted:

> *From its frontier beginning Phoenix was praised by dreamers, promoted by "boosters" and sold by hucksters. People were assured that the possibilities were limitless, and the future was whatever one wished to make of it. But the Valley also had particular characteristics that made it amenable to dreaming—which suggested a malleable environment. Abundant sun, level land and water—after the advent of "climate controls" like evaporative coolers and air conditioning—allowed migrants to remake the land with*

structures and landscaping into whatever they wished: a typical American suburb, a desert oasis, a tropical paradise, a ranch, or even a Midwestern lakeside community.[41]

Around the time that Ed semi-retired in 1949 at age fifty-six, he and Ruth bought a second home, a house with some acreage, in Scottsdale. One day, while out riding across the undeveloped desert near their new home, they came upon an area that they felt would make a perfect setting for Ed's vision: a large ranch dedicated to the breeding of Arabians. The Tweeds purchased this 160-acre parcel from Cheney for fifty dollars an acre, and Ed began to sketch out the plans for what he would call Brusally Ranch.

A brochure for Brusally Ranch from the 1960s demonstrates that, like many new residents, Ed used his land as an outlet for his creativity:

The Tweeds started their ranch with little more than two basic ingredients—sand and water. From an ample underground supply of the latter they filled a picturesque artificial lake which serves as a reservoir for widespread irrigation of permanent pastures and the beautifully kept lawns surrounding the buildings. The stables, tack room, trophy room, show ring and corrals are widely spaced to provide a maximum of light and air. Ruth and Ed built their own Spanish Colonial home a short hop, skip and a jump from the barns, allowing them to keep a close eye on what is going on.[42]

The ranch also featured a dairy, an aviary and, later, a racetrack and a covered riding arena—the first such structure in Arizona, allowing trainers to ride year round, even in the triple-digit Scottsdale summers.

When he was not busy creating his dream ranch, Ed was getting involved in the local community. He became a member of the Rotary Club's Scottsdale chapter, the Maricopa County Sheriff's Posse, the Masonic Temple and the El-Zaribah Shrine. He also made the acquaintance of other Arabian fanciers in the region, including Earle E. Hurlbutt, a California breeder who was the first president of the International Arabian Horse Association, which oversaw group activity related to Arabian horses, such as shows and clubs. Hurlbutt, who owned the well-known Polish Arabian stallion Witez II, encouraged Ed to establish an affiliated horse club in Arizona. Tweed contacted the twenty-odd Arabian breeders in Arizona, and in 1954, they met at the Westward Ho Hotel in Phoenix, where they formed the Arabian Horse Association of Arizona. Ed was the club's first president.

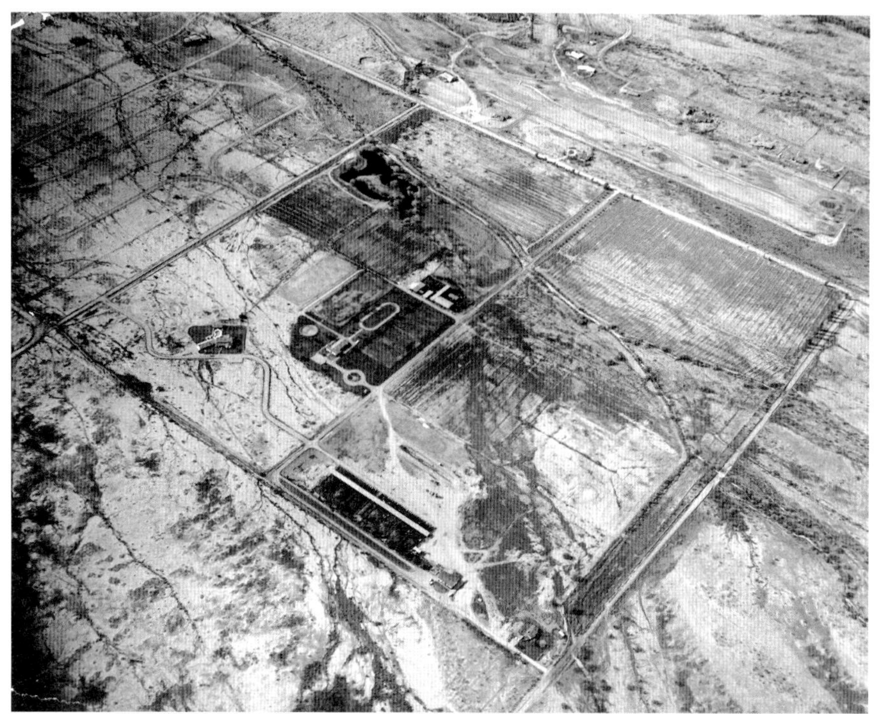

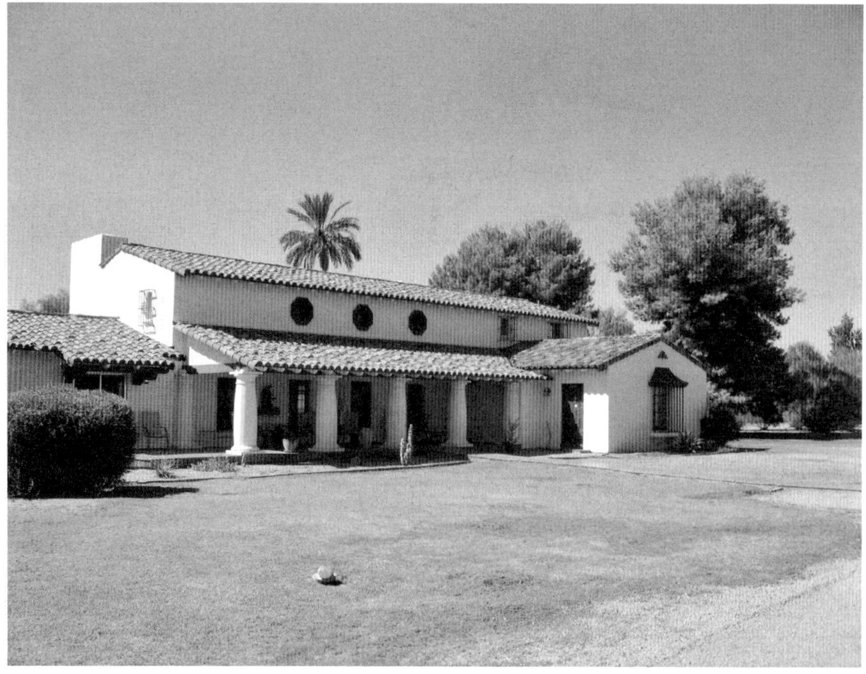

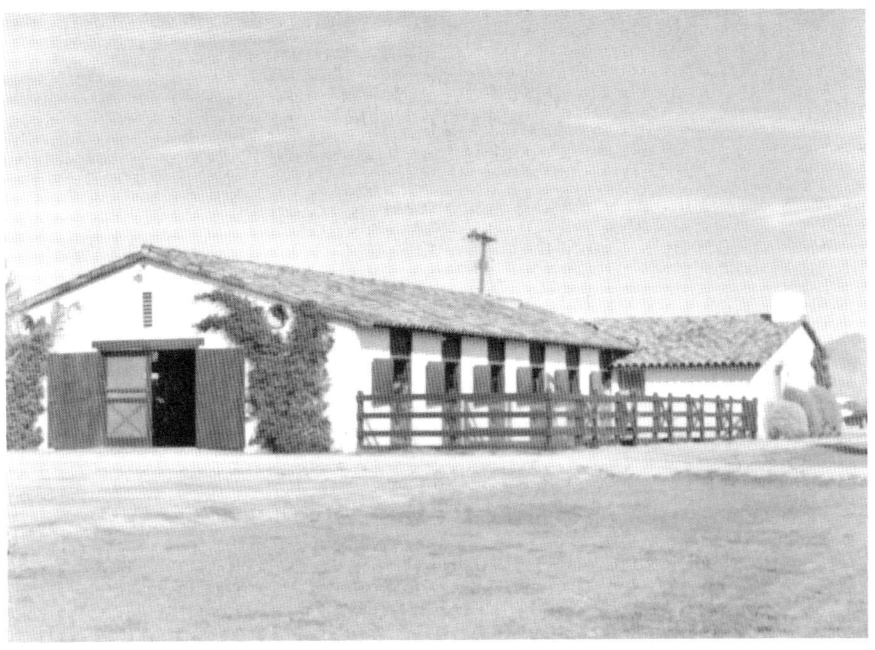

A Spanish Colonial–style barn designed by Ed Tweed. *Courtesy of Shelley Groom Trevor.*

Opposite, top: A 1960s aerial view of Brusally Ranch, looking southwest. The Tweed house is at center left. *Courtesy of Shelley Groom Trevor.*

Opposite, bottom: The Spanish Colonial–style home designed by Tweed for his Scottsdale ranch. *Courtesy of the author.*

Also that year, the nascent association held an unjudged exhibition of Arabians in an arena on the grounds of the Wrigley family's Arizona Biltmore Hotel in Phoenix. In February 1955, the association's first judged show was held, again at the Arizona Biltmore. Sponsored by the McCormicks, Tweeds and Wrigleys, and with Ed serving as the master of ceremonies, the show featured 135 horses from Arizona, California, Nevada, New Mexico, Texas and Utah. After a year's hiatus, in 1957, the show took place in a new locale, Paradise Park, not far from Brusally Ranch on land purchased by the McCormicks. This was the first time the show—now referred to by Arabian fanciers as the Scottsdale Arabian Show, or simply the Scottsdale Show—was actually held in Scottsdale.

For a number of years, the McCormicks and Tweeds provided hospitality for the show, with the McCormicks hosting a pre-show barbecue for exhibitors and the Tweeds holding a post-show luncheon. From such

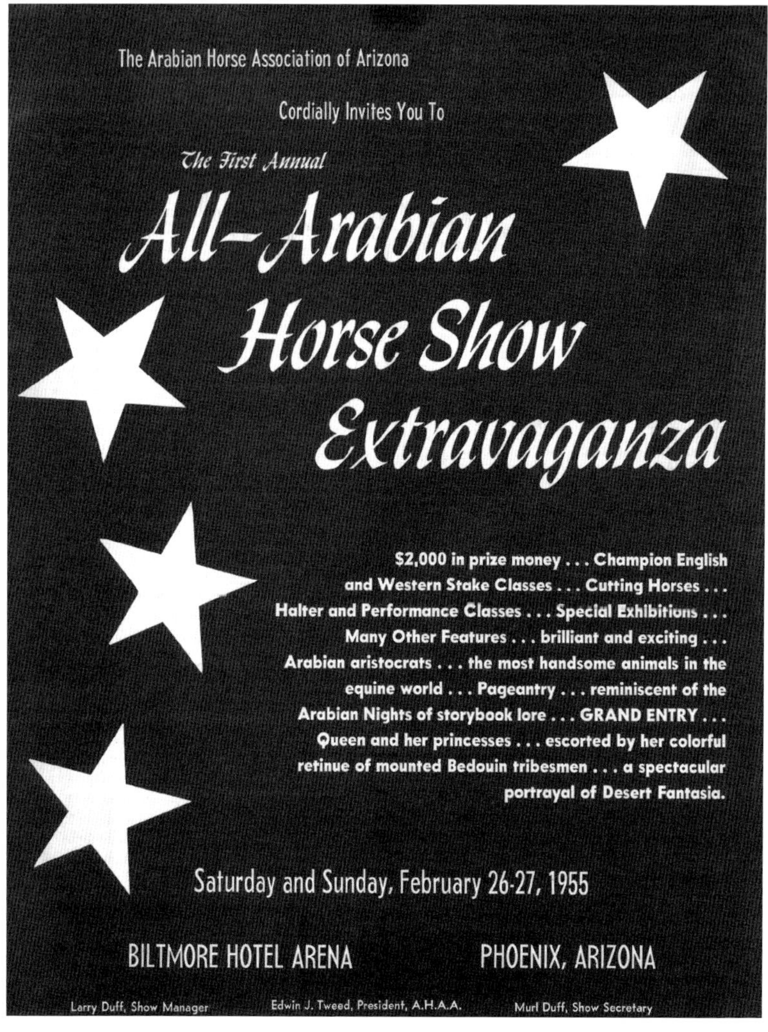

A rare copy of the 1955 program for an "All-Arabian Horse Show Extravaganza" held in Phoenix, Arizona. In 1957, the event was moved to Scottsdale, where it was renamed the Scottsdale All Arabian Horse Show and, later, simply the Scottsdale Arabian Horse Show. *Courtesy of the author.*

humble beginnings, the Scottsdale Show has evolved into an eleven-day event, one of the largest exhibitions of its kind in the world, attracting horses from across the United States and numerous foreign countries and contributing more than $50 million to the local economy. Over the decades, the show has become so important to Arabian breeders and exhibitors that a championship won at the Scottsdale Show, when combined with wins at the United States and Canadian national shows, is known as the Arabian Triple Crown.

In addition to building the local club and promoting the Scottsdale Show, Ed was steadily adding to his own herd of horses. He purchased well-bred mares from a number of breeders, including Robert B. Field of Washington; Albert W. Harris of Illinois; and L. Wayne Van Vleet of Colorado. Over the next few years, Tweed's band of broodmares grew to include daughters of the famous sires Ankar, Gamhuri, Hallany Mistanny, Hanraff, Raseyn, Rifage and Zarife.

To complement his mares, Ed searched the country for a high-quality stallion. Upon discovering that a three-year-old named Skorage had been named Grand Champion at an all-stallion show in Waterloo, Iowa, he arranged to see Skorage at the home of his breeder, Daniel C. Gainey, in Owatonna, Minnesota. Gainey had received his first Arabian in the 1930s, as a gift from the employees of Josten's, Inc., where he was chief executive officer. Gainey promptly bought two mares and soon became an Arabian breeder.[43] By the time Tweed and Gainey met in 1950, Gainey's breeding program had produced numerous champions. Ed recalled the day that he arrived at Gainey's farm: "It was bitter cold and the wind was blowing. I wrapped up in a horse blanket to watch the trainer lead out two stallions, Skorage and his full brother, two years old, Galimar. I bought Skorage, then and there."[44]

Skorage, a chestnut with four white legs and a blaze, was foaled on May 11, 1947. He grew to be fifteen hands tall and was described as "well proportioned," with

all the classic features we look for in the [Arabian] *breed—alert, wide-set intelligent eyes, slender muzzle and generous nostrils. His neck is arched and full to provide ample space for his windpipe. His chest cavity is full and broad allowing necessary room for heart and lungs. His back is straight, his withers perfectly formed for the snug fit of a saddle. He stands squarely on his four legs, long-sloping pasterns supplying the necessary spring to provide a comfortable ride. Judges of Arabian horse flesh have agreed that his conformation leaves little if anything to be desired.*[45]

Skorage was sired by Gaysar, which was a product of the Van Vleet breeding program. Like other horses bred by the Van Vleets, the athletically built chestnut was known as a "doing horse"—a magazine advertisement of the time shows him jumping an obstacle—and his offspring were likewise

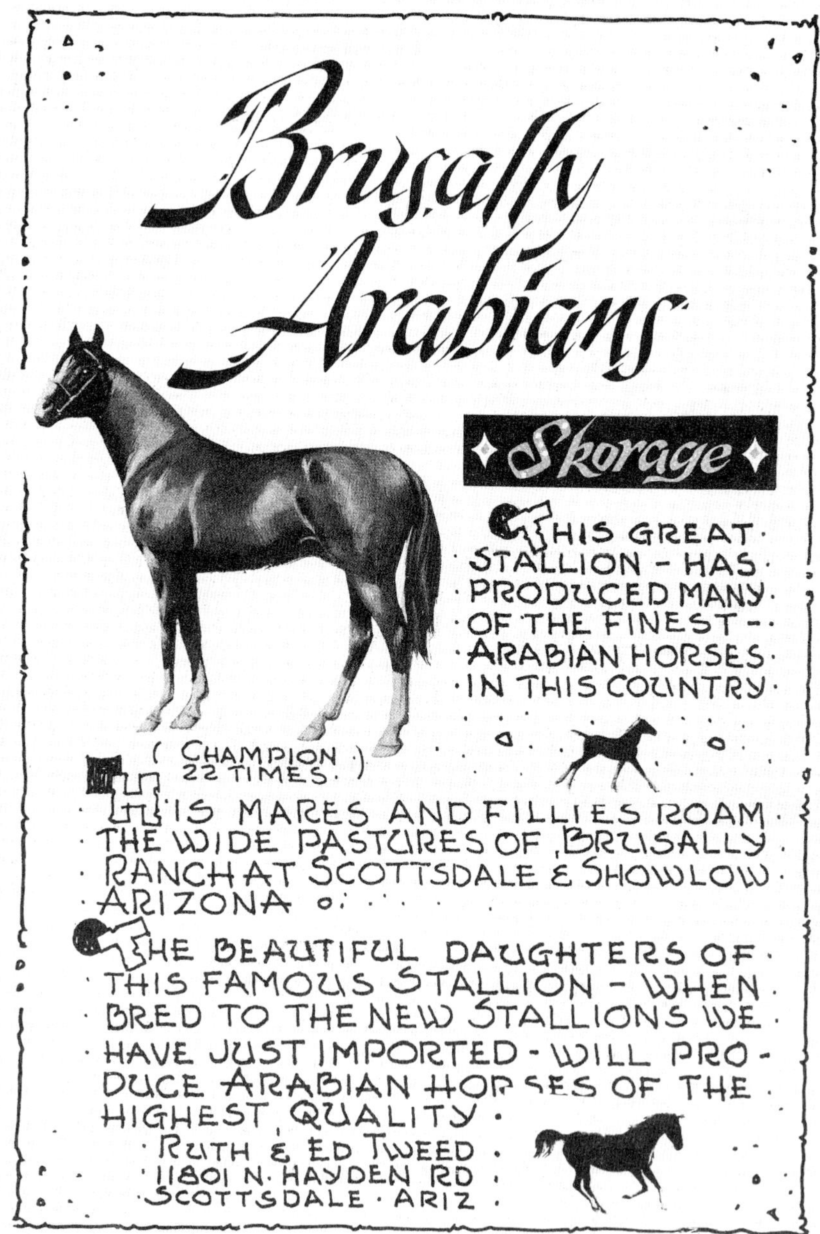

One of Tweed's hand-drawn advertisements. *Courtesy of Shelley Groom Trevor.*

talented. Gaysar's sire, Rifage, drove cattle on the Van Vleets' Lazy VV Ranch near Boulder, Colorado, at an elevation of 8,600 feet. Rifage was said to be

> *small, but with the ruggedness and grace of tens of hundreds of generations of pure Arabian breeding behind him…Rifage weighs 850 pounds. Frequently, his rider and equipment will weigh 250 or 275 pounds, or one third of gallant Rifage's own poundage. He doesn't falter—he doesn't stumble on that trail. When the pack train stops to "blow" in the rare air, Rifage disdains the opportunity to catch his breath.[46]*

When Rifage wasn't out riding the range, he was used in the breeding shed, siring a number of national winners, including Rominna, U.S. National Champion Mare, and U.S. National Top Ten winners Rishima, Shihada and Sulyman.

Skorage's dam, Rageyma, was bred by Roger A. Selby, a Portsmouth, Ohio shoe manufacturer, from stock he imported from England beginning in 1928. Her sire, Mirage, was also the paternal grandsire of Gaysar, Skorage's sire. Mirage was bred in the Arabian desert by the Sebaa Anazeh tribe and was said to have been "selected to head the stud of King Faisal of Iraq, who paid $2500 for him as a young horse."[47] He was purchased in a 1923 Tattersalls auction by Lady Wentworth (Judith Blunt-Lytton) of Crabbet Arabian Stud, Sussex, England, and in 1926 won a championship at the Richmond Royal horse show. Cecil Covey, who had been a stud manager at Crabbet Stud, recalled that Mirage had a "great character, very exhilarating ride having been ridden in the desert in battle. Quiet and tractable to handle at all times. Very compact, good head and very large eye, tail set high and carried well."[48] After his 1930 importation by Selby, Mirage sired only twenty-six foals, but his male line exerts a great influence worldwide, particularly through his descendant Bay-Abi, the cornerstone of Sheila Varian's Arabian breeding program in California. According to the Varian Arabians website, "70% of the show horses winning today carry Varian blood"—and the vast majority of those horses have at least one line to Varian's herd sire, Bay-Abi, and thus to Mirage.[49] One breeder who was not a fan of Mirage's bloodlines was Tweed's good friend Bazy Tankersley of Al-Marah Arabians, who told historian Mary Jane Parkinson in 1998 that she had "weeded out" the Mirage bloodlines from her herd, as these horses "too often did not produce heads to my liking, but I regretted giving up the wonderful dispositions."[50]

Rageyma's dam, Kareyma, was bred by Crabbet Stud and imported by Selby in 1928. Sired by the handsome stallion Naseem, which Lady Wentworth had sold to the USSR for a large sum, Kareyma "was a very correct and beautiful grey mare who was [trained] as a five-gaited riding horse. During her show career, Kareyma won first place both in hand and under saddle at the Ohio State Fair in 1932 and second in the National Arabian five-gaited championship in 1934."[51] Later, Kareyma became known as an excellent producer of breeding stallions and broodmares—including Skorage's dam, Rageyma—and her name is often found in today's pedigrees. In addition to Skorage and his brother Galimar (sire of one national winner), Rageyma produced nine other foals, including the influential stallion Geym, sire of four national winners; the great broodmare Gajala, dam of five national winners and creator of a dynasty for Gainey; Gallant, U.S. National Top Ten Trail; and Gageyma, dam of one national winner.

Clearly, Skorage had what it took, genetically, to excel at whatever Tweed wanted him to do. As writer Marian K. Carpenter noted:

> *Tweed believed in promoting Arabian horses at every opportunity—and the Tweed horses in particular. With Harold and Florence Daugherty as trainers—and later Earl Craig, Charlie Carter, and Steve Spalding—Tweed sent the spunky chestnut stallion on the road. He became the star attraction at horse shows, parades, and special exhibitions all over the country for well over a decade. The stallion became well known to horse lovers across the nation, no matter what their breed affiliation, and influenced scores of people to purchase purebred and Half-Arabian horses. Skorage was simply a superb ambassador for the entire Arabian breed.*[52]

A brochure, penned by magazine writer Ed Ellinger about the ranch and dating to the early 1960s, indicated that Skorage had won twenty-two halter championships at shows in California, Colorado, Iowa, Missouri, Nebraska, New Mexico, Texas and Utah, as well as 112 blue ribbons in halter and performance classes. Since Skorage continued to be shown until 1966, he undoubtedly had even more wins to his credit. In fact, he was the 1956 high-scoring horse among all breeds, according to the American Horse Shows Association. And, as Ellinger observed, the versatile Skorage was "shown in almost any show class open to purebred Arabian stallions. That would include English pleasure, Western pleasure, Native Costume, Parade Horse, Trail Horse, Three-gaited and any of the driving classes."[53]

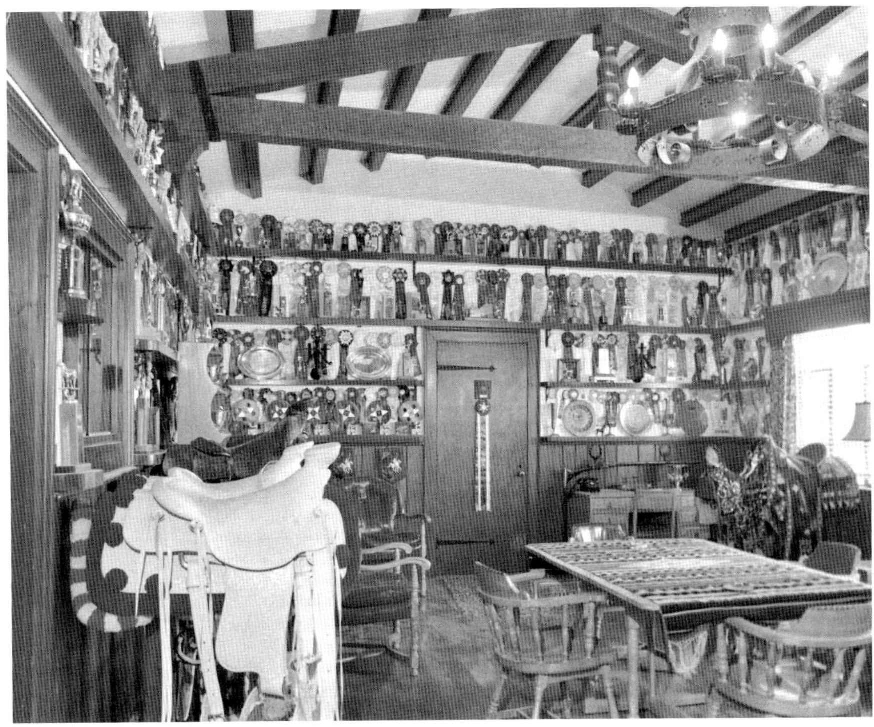

The Brusally Ranch tack and trophy room in the 1960s. *Courtesy of Shelley Groom Trevor.*

When Skorage wasn't showing or breeding mares, Tweed arranged for him to appear in advertisements for both local and national businesses, including a 1960 color brochure for Ford Motor Company, which also featured humorist and singer Tennessee Ernie Ford, who hosted a television variety show sponsored by the car manufacturer. Whenever a local magazine ran an article about horses, particularly Arabians, it was rare that Skorage was not included. If out-of-town breeders expressed interest in Skorage, Tweed invited them to come to the ranch to meet the stallion and his foals. Skorage became so famous that many well-wishers sent the Tweeds portraits of their stallion in a variety of media, while others made pilgrimages to see him. For example, when a young equine artist named Emilie Touraine moved to the Scottsdale area in the early 1960s, "she went immediately to Brusally Ranch to see Skorage—just as an art teacher, on arriving in Paris, might head at once for the Louvre to see Mona Lisa."[54]

By the early 1960s, Skorage's sons and daughters—the majority of which were chestnut, like their sire—were beginning to make their mark in the show ring. Between 1961 and 1964, Skorage's son Pulque and daughters Skorata

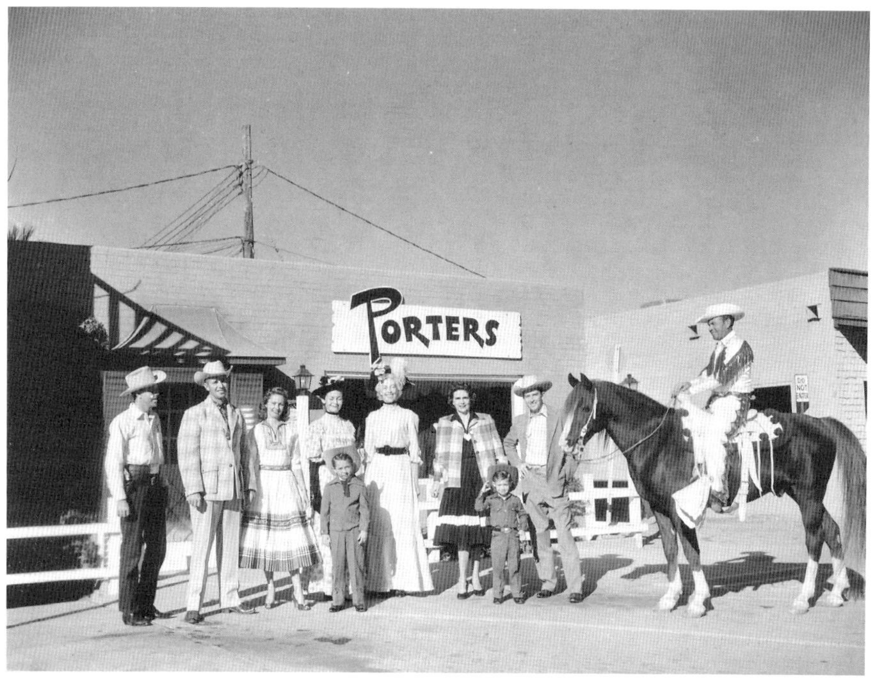

Skorage, ridden by Harold Daugherty, in an advertisement for Porters' Western Wear, Scottsdale, Arizona, late 1950s. *Courtesy of Shelley Groom Trevor.*

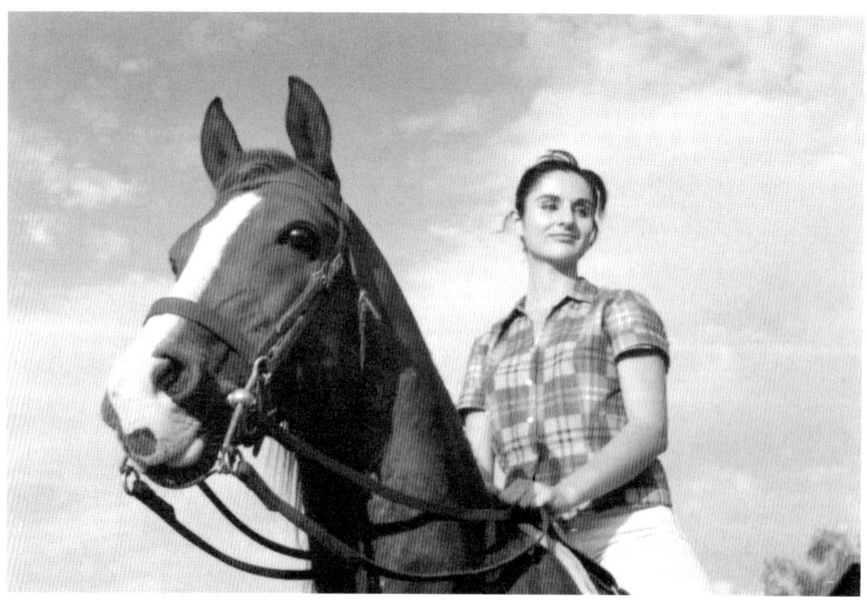

Artist Emilie "Rainbow" Touraine on Skorage, 1962. *Courtesy of Shelley Groom Trevor.*

and Skor-Enne racked up a total of eight national titles. Ultimately, Skorage would sire seventy-one foals, of which five would become national winners and twenty would be show champions in numerous disciplines.[55] Tweed was not content to stop there. Like any good horse breeder, he was looking toward the next generation, in which Skorage's daughters would be bred to high-quality stallions of Tweed's own choosing.

In 1960, Ed's neighbor, Arabian breeder Robert Aste, acquired a well-bred, twenty-two-year-old Arabian stallion named Lotnik. Like Witez II, the stallion owned by Tweed's friend Earle Hurlbutt, Lotnik was born in Poland, seized by Germany during the Second World War and then confiscated by American forces along with several other Polish Arabians.[56] Lotnik and Witez II were different from many typical American-bred Arabians of the time—both were of angular build, with more prominent withers and strong loins. Purebred Arabians had been bred in Poland since at least

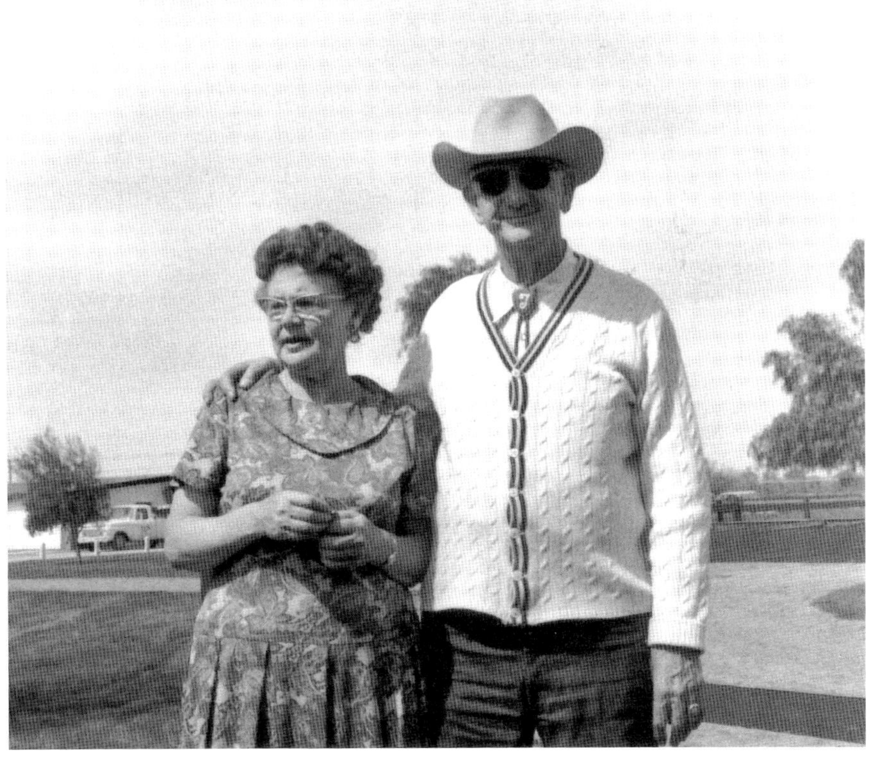

Tweed and his friend Gladys Brown Edwards, Arabian horse historian and artist. *Courtesy of Shelley Groom Trevor.*

the early 1800s, and breeders there had produced horses according to stringent criteria, including "nobility, beauty, great vitality, stamina, a vital but placid temperament, consistency and harmony of shape, flexibility of movement, perfect tissue quality, good metabolism, an ability to reliably pass on its features to its offspring, and versatility in uses whether saddled or in harness."[57] Furthermore, Polish Arabians were generally only distantly related to many American-bred Arabians of the time and thus could bring in new bloodlines.

Tweed and Aste were not the only breeders who were intrigued by Polish Arabians. In the late 1950s, Patricia Lindsay, a young Arabian breeder residing in England, "had come to the conclusion that it would be a good thing to introduce some fresh blood into British Arab breeding, and she decided to look around on the Continent. As she speaks fluent Polish, she set off for Poland. What started as a sightseeing tour turned into a [horse-]buying spree."[58] She then began helping other English breeders procure Polish Arabians. After Lindsay published an article about her new acquisitions in the *Arab Horse Society News*, Arabian horse historian Gladys Brown Edwards contacted her on behalf of a number of American breeders, such as Raymond J. Ashton, Ines M. Doner, Frisco Mari, H.H. Reese and John M. Rogers, who wanted their own Polish Arabians. With the help of Lindsay and Edwards, Aste became the first breeder to import Polish Arabians to Scottsdale. Other local Arabian fanciers, including Tweed, took note of these exciting new horses, and soon a veritable "Polish invasion" was underway in Arizona.

Chapter 3

LITTLE POLAND

In 1963, as Ed Tweed approached his seventieth birthday, he had no idea that he was also embarking on the most ambitious, productive decade of his life. That February, the champion stallion at the Scottsdale Show was a Polish import named Muzulmanin, which piqued Tweed's fancy not only for his charisma and correct conformation but also for his color and markings—chestnut with plenty of white, like his beloved Skorage. Ed immediately arranged for Muzulmanin to be bred to his half-Polish mare Samara, whose dam, Przepiorka, was the first Polish Arabian registered in the Arabian Horse Registry of America upon her importation in 1937 by General J.M. Dickinson. Tweed also instructed his trainer at the time, Steve Spalding, and ranch manager, H. Dean Cantrell, to prepare for a trip to the Netherlands, England and Poland, with the intention of importing some Arabians—particularly some from Poland—with the help of Patricia Lindsay. Spalding, who had worked for Tweed since late 1961, was a study in contrasts: this thirty-year-old marine staff sergeant who had served in the Korean War was also a talented, sensitive rider and trainer whose love for horses was noted by his friend artist Emilie Touraine.[59]

During the roughly six-week period that Spalding traveled in Europe (Cantrell having returned to the United States after three weeks), he had the opportunity to meet a number of prominent horse breeders, including H. Musgrave Clark (onetime owner of the influential stallion Skowronek), Cecil Covey, Margaret Evans, Pieter Houtappel and Lady Anne Lytton, granddaughter of Wilfrid and Lady Anne Blunt, founders of the Crabbet

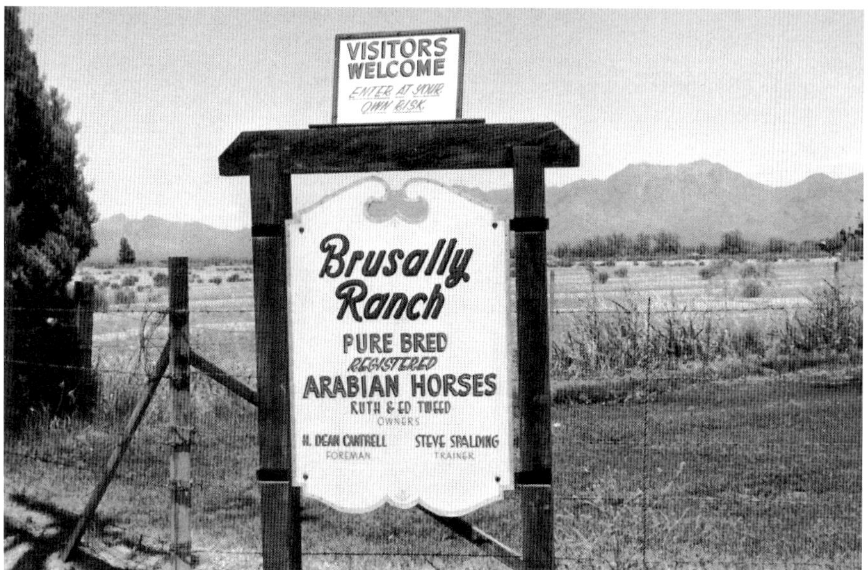

The Brusally Ranch sign, early 1960s, showing the names of Steve Spalding and Dean Cantrell. *Courtesy of Shelley Groom Trevor.*

Stud. In Poland, Spalding and Cantrell visited a number of the state-run Arabian breeding farms, as well as the racetrack in Warsaw, looking for quality horses to ship home to Brusally. Negotiations with the Poles took longer than expected, and Spalding made a few trips back and forth between Poland and England. While in England, Spalding encountered a Russian Arabian horse importer/exporter and art collector named Peter Provatoroff, whose wife, Nina Vanna, had appeared in a number of British films in the 1920s and whose brother was a Russian icon specialist for Christie's auction house in London.[60]

Bred at the USSR's Tersk Stud, Russian Arabians shared some bloodlines with both Polish Arabians and the horses bred by the Crabbet Stud. Spalding, who had the proverbial eye for a horse, had admired the Russian Arabians owned by Evans, and when he saw the Russian stallion Park at Provatoroff's Crittenden Manor in Kent, he quickly snapped him up. Park, a race winner in the USSR, had been graded "elite" by Tersk; his dam was a sister of Pietuszok, making Park an "uncle" of Orzel. Spalding also agreed to buy some Russian mares for Tweed through Provatoroff. Unfortunately, because of the Arabian Horse Registry of America's Cold War–influenced policy at the time regarding Russian-bred Arabian horses, Tweed was unable to register the three imported Russian horses that Spalding acquired for him. That meant

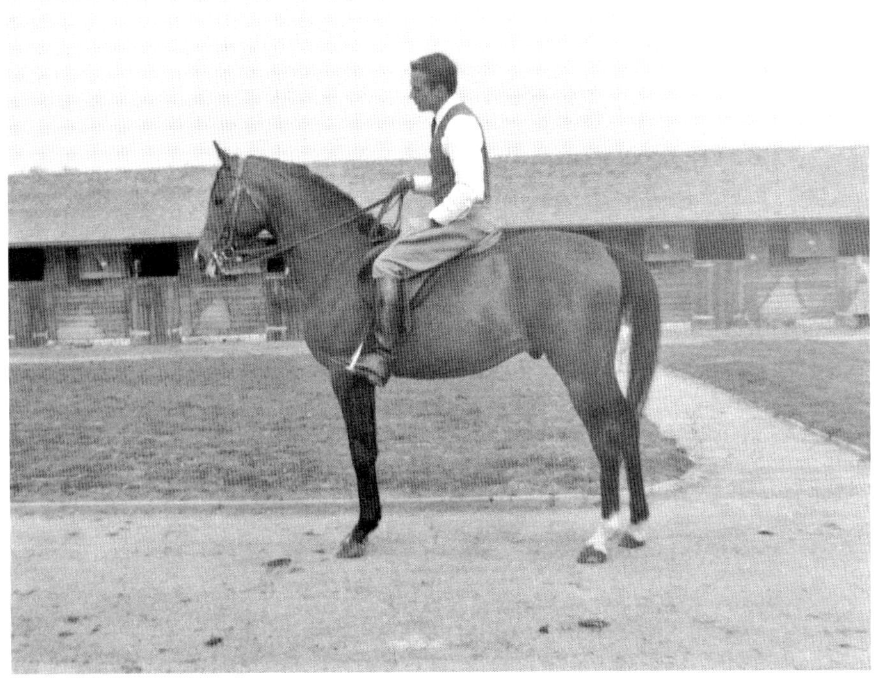

Steve Spalding astride Park, a Russian-bred stallion he imported from England for Ed Tweed in 1963. Park was closely related to Orzel; his dam, Ptashka, was a sister of Orzel's sire, Pietuszok. *Courtesy of Shelley Groom Trevor.*

they could not be shown or used to breed registerable, purebred foals. In fact, it was not until 1978 that the American registry finally allowed the registration of Russian-bred Arabians; by then, Park had been dead for four years, and Tweed's Russian mares Napaika and Palmira were aged horses.[61]

In early May, Spalding was back in Poland making the final arrangements to ship Tweed's fourteen Polish Arabians by air to America. During that time—on May 5, to be exact—the celebrated Polish broodmare Ofirka gave birth to her final foal, Orzel, at Janow Podlaski Stud. It is unknown whether Spalding heard about Orzel's birth, but he did know of Ofirka, and he certainly knew about Orzel's sire, Pietuszok—and not only because of purchasing the stallion Park. Spalding had told Tweed the previous month that he was "angling" to buy a two-year-old daughter of Pietuszok—Carmen—from Musgrave Clark: "[T]he filly is a bit large for his standards—but he likes her color. Nevertheless, I think there may be a chance he shall sell her."[62] (Clark did sell her that year, but not to Tweed.)

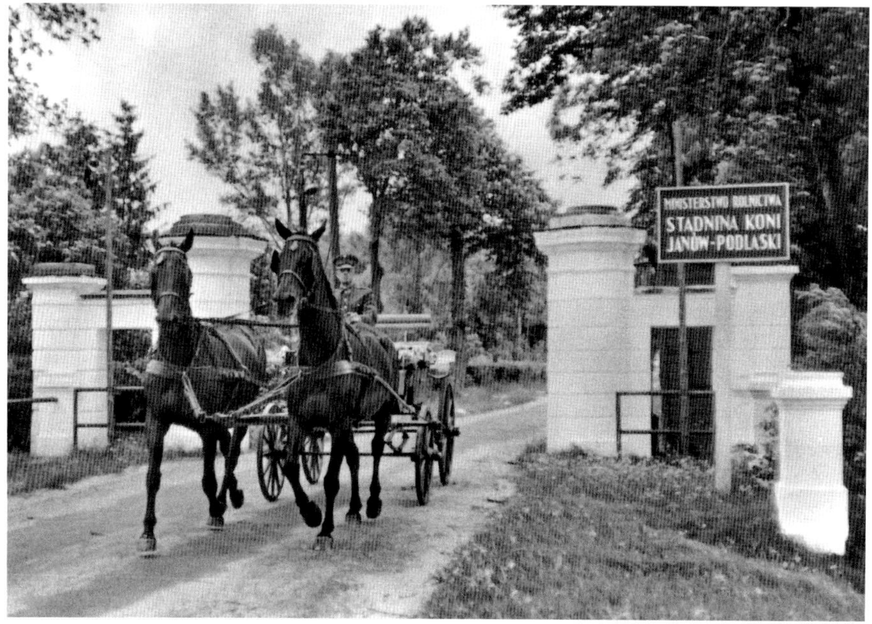

The gate outside Janow Podlaski State Stud (established 1817), where Orzel was foaled in May 1963. *Courtesy of Shelley Groom Trevor.*

Another relative of Orzel's that interested Spalding was Orszak, a seven-year-old son of Ofirka. He noted that Orszak was a "big horse, but of classic type, a great performer. Pat [Lindsay] says he will amaze the world. (She will have to locate him as he is not for sale.)"[63] That was the last time Spalding mentioned Orszak. He may not have known that Orszak was being used in the breeding of half-Arabians at Poland's Albigowa Stud. Arabian race breeding in America might have turned out quite differently if Spalding had found and purchased Orszak, a tall, chestnut, race-winning son of Ofirka; perhaps Tweed would not have felt the need to import his half brother Orzel in 1967.

On May 16, Tweed's fourteen Polish Arabians traveled from Warsaw to New York, and the three Russian Arabians left England the next month, sailing on the SS *Crux*. The shipment from Poland included the mares Abhazja, Algorina, Almeria (registered in America as Almeriaa), Basta, Chlosta, Daszenka, Genua, Gontyna, Miroluba, Nawojka, Rifata and Warna and the stallions Czester and Gwiazdor. Tweed also bought two more Polish-bred stallions, Centaur and Faraon, which had been imported by other American breeders.

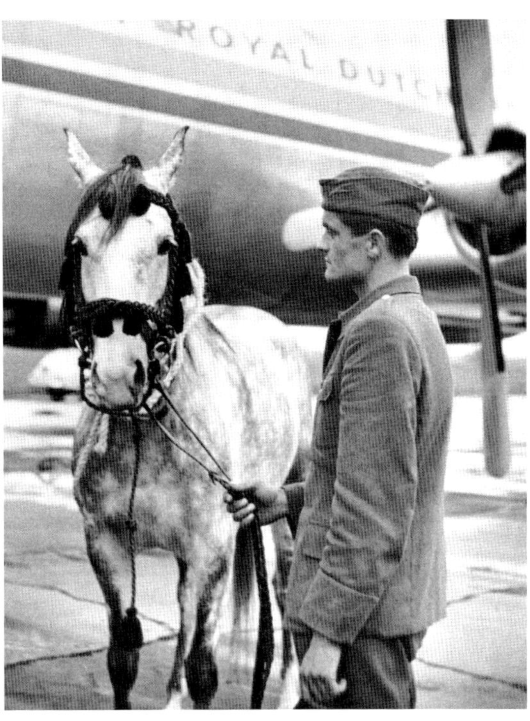

Right: The mare Nawojka, one of fourteen Arabians purchased by Tweed from Poland in 1963, stands with a groom by the airplane that would fly the horses from Warsaw to New York. *Courtesy of Shelley Groom Trevor.*

Below: Brusally trainer Steve Spalding and the Polish mare Genua arrive in New York, 1963. Note the nametag braided into her mane. *Courtesy of Shelley Groom Trevor.*

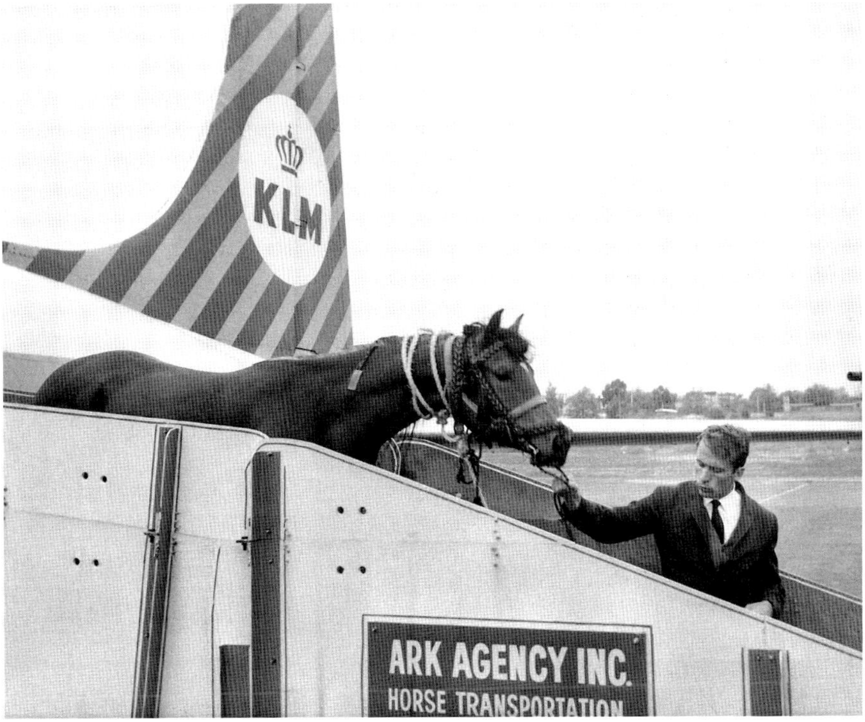

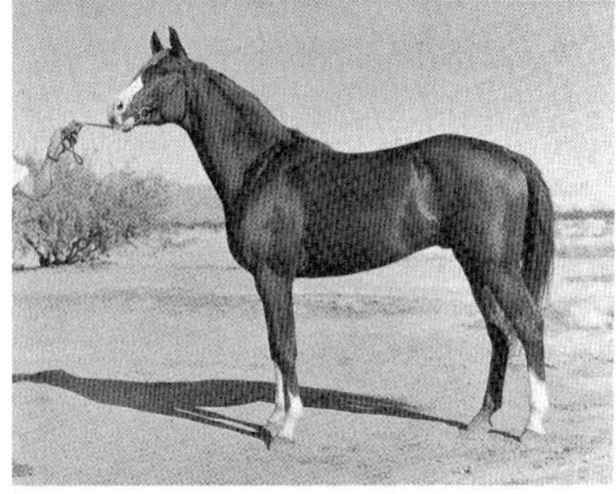

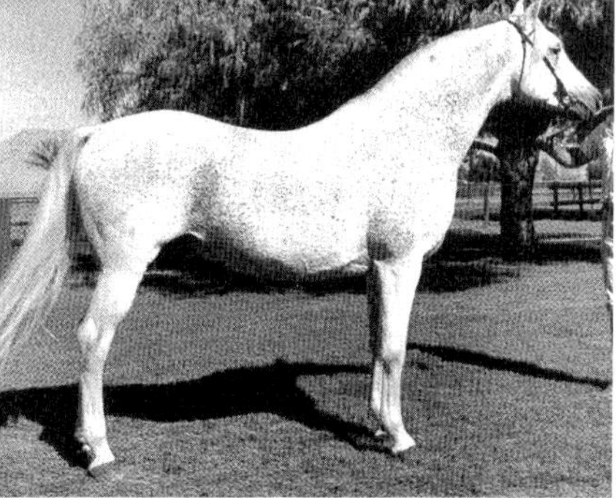

Brusally Ranches

Breed to these great imported Polish stallions and obtain the tremendous influence of this Polish Arabian blood — achieving the utmost in increased size, classic beauty, stamina, intelligence, gentleness, plus conformation that will win for you in the shows.

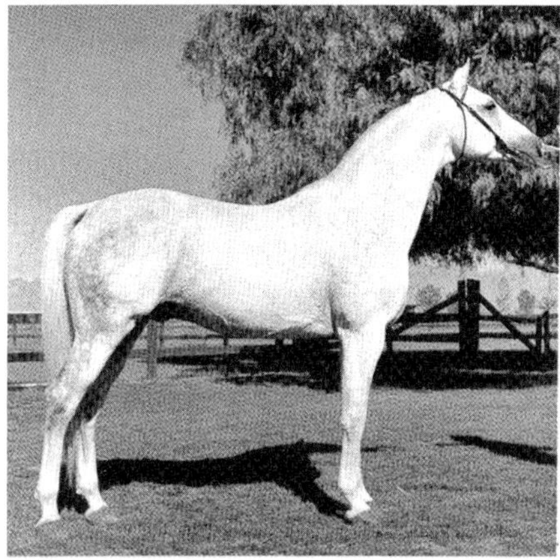
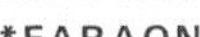

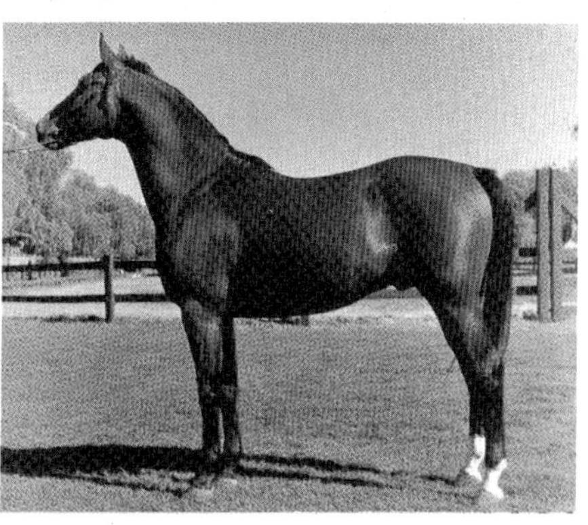

All of us at Brusally Ranch thank each and every one who came to our 2nd Production Sale — and a special thanks to those who purchased our horses. We wish for you much success with them!

Ruth and Ed Tweed, Owners   Charles Carter, Manager
11801 N. Hayden Road, Scottsdale and Show Low, Arizona   948-6420

An advertisement featuring four of Tweed's champion Polish stallions. *Courtesy of Shelley Groom Trevor.*

Polish horses, including Tweed's, began to dominate Arabian competitions. For example, starting with Muzulmanin in 1963, the stallion championship at the Scottsdale Show was won by a Polish import or a half-Polish stallion every year until 1971. The Brusally stallion Gwiazdor was named a Canadian National Top Ten Stallion in 1964. The next year, his stablemate Czester was named champion stallion at the Scottsdale Show, as well as U.S. and Canadian National Top Ten Stallion; he then followed those wins with another Canadian National Top Ten title in 1966. And the Brusally stallion Faraon also gained national recognition when he was named a Canadian National Top Ten Stallion in 1965. Additionally, all three stallions won many other awards at local and regional shows.

By 1964, Tweed's ranch manager H. Dean Cantrell had moved on to another management position at Robert Aste's nearby Desert Arabian Ranch. Trainer Steve Spalding—who had big dreams for Brusally but was perhaps too sensitive a rider and trainer to be truly competitive for such a large operation—relocated to San Saba, Texas, where he served for a while as the U.S. Marine Corps' supervisor of an Arabian horse training operation. Spalding later was the manager and trainer for Paragon Arabians of New Hudson, Michigan, for whom he trained the imported Polish stallion Werbor. In fact, when Spalding showed Werbor to a 1970 U.S. National Top Ten Stallion title, he was competing against Orzel, which was not named to the Top Ten that year. Another horse in Spalding's care during that time was Paragon Czestina, a daughter of Czester and Algorina, both imported by Spalding for Brusally in 1963. Tweed's granddaughter Shelley Groom Trevor met Spalding only once, in the early 1970s, at a horse show, where she learned that he was no longer training horses. Spalding died in 1976, at age forty-three.

In 1964, Spalding was replaced as Brusally's trainer by Denis Scully, who first worked with Thoroughbred racehorses in his native Ireland before he switched to Arabians. Scully and a van full of show horses crisscrossed the country, culminating in what became known as Brusally's "big year"—1966—when four Brusally horses, Aabeebe, Czester, Rocarro and Star of Erka, won at the U.S. National Championship Show. At Brusally, work was begun on an indoor riding arena, and in early 1967, timed to coincide with the Scottsdale Show, Tweed held the city's first Arabian horse auction. The sale, which brought in $104,600—quite a tidy sum for the time—consisted mainly of young horses sired by Tweed's new Polish stallions and out of his Polish mares, as well as a few by Skorage out of mares of either Polish or domestic breeding. Of the thirty-eight lots, the highest sellers were of pure Polish breeding. Because of this interest in Polish horses, "Brusally shifted from a breeding program centered on Skorage's Mirage lines to one dedicated to pure Polish lineage. The ranch was dubbed 'Little Poland.'"[64]

Meanwhile, as Tweed learned more about Polish horse breeding and management practices, including the use of racing as a way to evaluate horses' athletic potential, he became interested in racing his own Polish Arabians. Dixie Ryan noted in her profile of Tweed, "He found that since 1926 extreme emphasis has been placed [by Polish breeders] on racing abilities. Not only track records but training records, recovery after races and many other factors."[65]

After Tweed's 1963 importation of horses, representatives of the Polish State stud farms kept in contact with him, sending him lists and

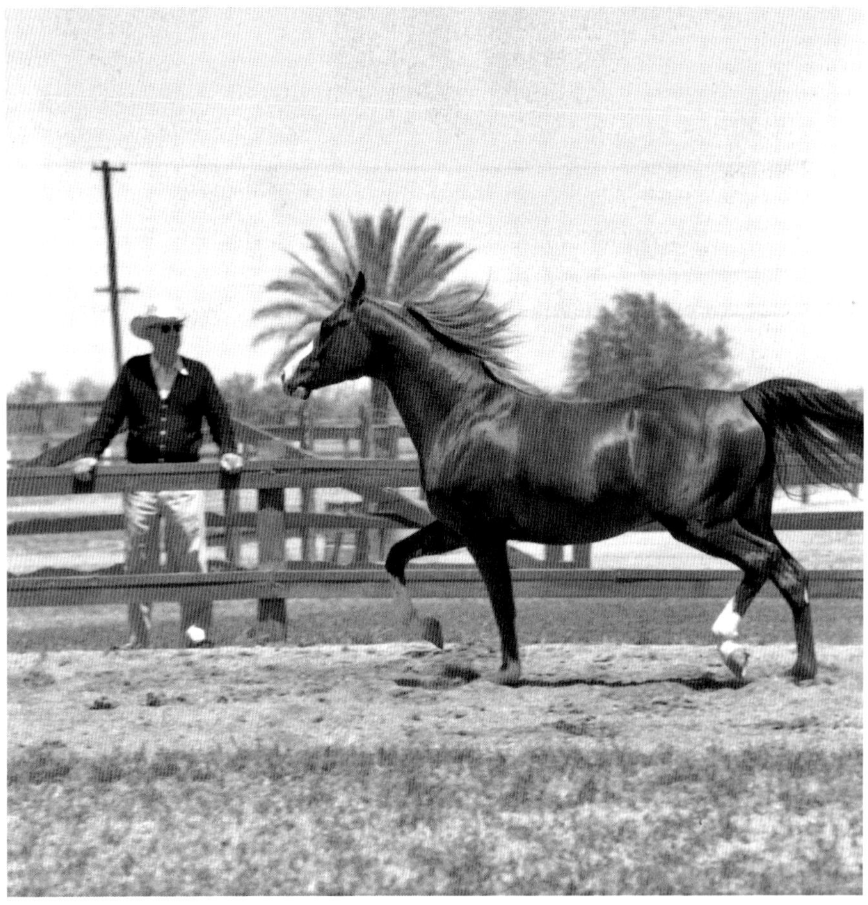

Tweed watches Orzel cavort in a paddock at Brusally Ranch. *Courtesy of Shelley Groom Trevor.*

photographs of horses for sale. One such list, dated December 9, 1966, featured seven stallions for sale: Almifar, Ego, Flis, Gazda, Orzel, Pien and Ruszt, ranging in price from $7,000 to $14,000. Orzel, the second-highest-priced horse on the list, was the only horse that Tweed purchased. The highest-priced horse, Pien, which was closely related to Orzel through his dam, had handed Orzel's older sister, Orla, the only defeat of her racing career. According to Gladys Brown Edwards, Pien was "a very flashy horse with a high bold trot…an eyecatcher, and was [eventually] sold to a circus."[66] Pien had no foals.

In April 1967, Tweed sent Scully to Poland to purchase a group of horses for racing, breeding and resale. Unlike Spalding, Scully wrote no reports to Tweed about the horses he saw; the only records he left consisted of one- and two-word, barely legible notes on lists of horses provided by the Poles, as well as some brief cables. After spending weeks looking at horses at Janow Podlaski Stud, Michalow Stud and the racetrack in Warsaw, Scully chose eight mares and two stallions. The mares were Bulawa, Cerera, Lawenda (and her filly Laura), Manna, Paleta, Prowizja, Salina (registered as Salinaa in the United States) and Wislica. The two stallions chosen by Scully—Orzel and Zbrucz—would prove to be "game changers" for Brusally, both as show horses and, later, as sires. In fact, the genetic intertwining of these two stablemates and rivals would ultimately result in what breeders call a "good nick"—a combination of bloodlines that consistently results in particularly high-quality offspring, such as the famous Nasrullah-Princequillo nick, which produced Secretariat, Seattle Slew, Mill Reef and others. In the case of Orzel and Zbrucz, the nick worked both ways, whether Orzel was bred to Zbrucz's daughters or vice versa. But for the moment, Ed wasn't looking toward the far-off future; rather, he was solidly in the present, preparing to send Orzel, which was said to have been favored to win the 1967 Polish Derby, off to the races in America.

Chapter 4

LIKE AN EAGLE

When four-year-old Orzel stepped off the van that had brought him from New York to his new home at Brusally Ranch, Ed Tweed was immediately struck by his new acquisition's tremendous physique and size; already over fifteen hands when he arrived in America, Orzel would eventually grow to be nearly sixteen hands tall. It probably didn't hurt, either, that he was a chestnut with white markings, like Ed's avowed favorite, Skorage, and Muzulmanin, the Polish horse that had turned Tweed's head at the 1963 Scottsdale Show. Shelley Groom Trevor recalled that the young Orzel was lean, hard and racing fit, "graceful as a deer but powerful and quite a handful."[67] Tweed's friend Gladys Brown Edwards proclaimed, "This magnificent red chestnut has as grand a forehand as one might ever see, with long shoulder, arched neck and breedy [refined] head."[68] And the well-known racing trainer Chuck Tolbert admired Orzel not only for his racing prowess but also because he had attributes that were lacking in the majority of horses at the time: "excellent size, depth, substance, and bone."[69]

Orzel's athletic conformation could have been predicted from his impeccable racing pedigree, a blend of the best of Russian, Hungarian, French, Polish and Crabbet breeding. His sire, the unraced Pietuszok—which Tweed appears to have tried, unsuccessfully, to purchase after he had acquired Orzel—was descended through his male line from the influential Koheilan I. This gray stallion, born in 1922 at Hungary's Babolna Stud and later exported to Poland, was said to be "a compact, strongly-built horse, correct throughout, and is noted as a sire of three winners of the Arab

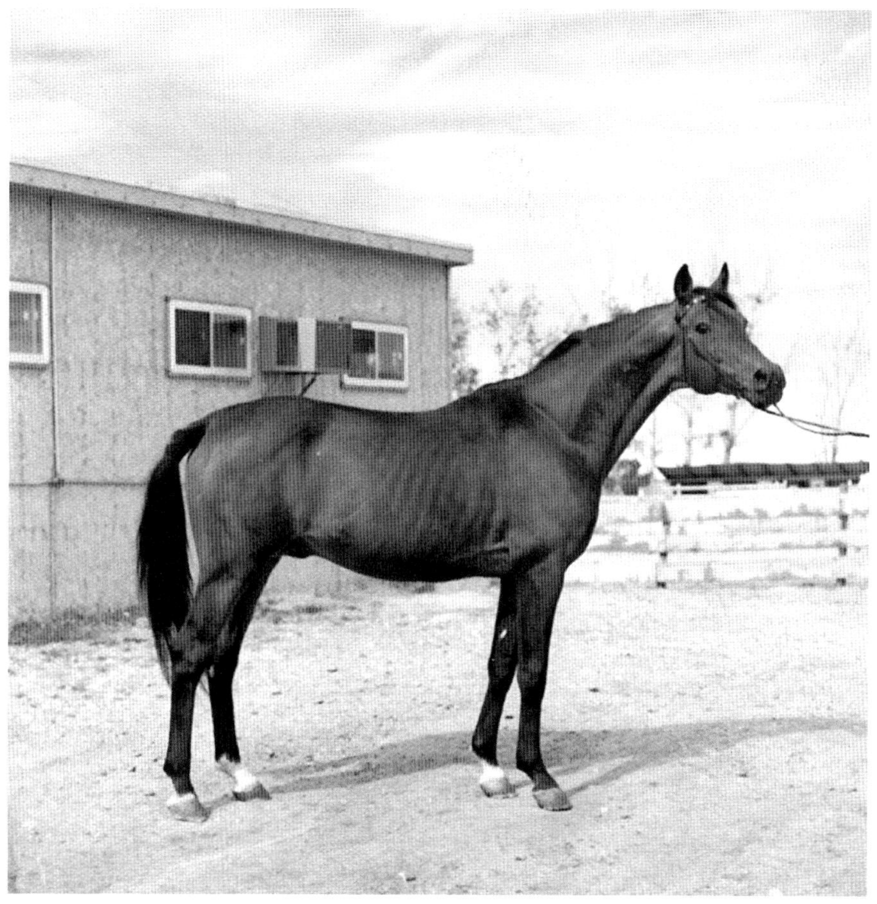

The Russian-bred stallion Pietuszok was the sire of Orzel. *Courtesy of Shelley Groom Trevor.*

Derby in Poland, where he was for several years the leading sire of money winners."[70]

Koheilan I's Polish-born son Piolun, a chestnut born in 1934, was removed from Poland in 1939 by the Soviet army to the USSR's Tersk Stud in southwestern Russia. Piolun had been a race winner in Poland, and he passed on his prowess to his Russian offspring, including the Russian Derby winner and major sire Priboj, grandsire of Orzel. Just as Piolun resulted from an outcross of Hungarian and Polish bloodlines, Priboj, too, was an outcross: his dam, Rissalma, had been bred by Lady Anne and Wilfrid Blunt of the Crabbet Stud and was purchased by Tersk in 1936. Priboj, a tall chestnut, was a true sire of athletes; in addition to many race winners and track-record setters, he sired the stallion Sport, which competed in three-day events (dressage, cross-country and show jumping) and won against other breeds, including Thoroughbreds. John Schiewe, Arabian breeder and researcher, suggests that the tall chestnut Orzel was a "throwback" to Priboj, "particularly with respect to the ratio of forearm to cannon [length]."[71] Priboj also figured in the pedigrees of the three Russian-bred horses—Palmira, Napaika and Park—imported by Tweed in 1963 (see Chapter 3). Palmira was a maternal granddaughter of Priboj, while Napaika was by Pomeranets, a son of Priboj and Mammona, a daughter of Ofir. And Park's dam, Ptashka, a daughter of Priboj and Taktika, was one of several siblings of Pietuszok.

After Pietuszok was sold to Poland, he was bred to purebred mares at Albigowa Stud during the years 1958 through 1960 and at Janow Podlaski Stud between 1961 and 1962. From 1963 to 1967, he sired only part-bred foals, including warmbloods, at the Pruchna and Liski Studs, and in 1968, he was returned to Janow Stud for purebred breeding. In 1973, breeder George W. Allen imported Pietuszok to Canada, where he sired his last six foals. Pietuszok died in November 1974 at age twenty.[72] Pietuszok left no foals in the USSR, the Russians apparently preferring to use his brother, Topol, a Russian Triple Crown winner and himself an excellent sire. In Poland, Pietuszok was well regarded as a sire of racehorses; his get captured the Polish Derby twice, the Oaks twice and the Criterium three times. His daughters were valued by Polish breeders as broodmares, but only one of his sons, Wosk, was used at stud in Poland and only briefly. The influence of Pietuszok as a sire of sires was not fully appreciated until his sons in the United States and Canada began to sire their own top-quality offspring.

In addition to Orzel, Pietuszok's stallion sons include (in order of birth) Bajram, Wosk, Gaypolka, Cypr, Hussar, Pietuszok Dwa, Pietrak and Black Russian, all of which stood at stud in North America. Bajram, a race winner in Poland, later was named Canadian National Champion Stallion and won two other national titles (in cutting and stock). He sired six national winners from ninety-six purebred foals, as well as at least two race winners.[73] Bajram appears in the pedigrees of contemporary horses primarily through his many national winner–producing daughters.

Wosk, which inexplicably finished last in his only race against Orzel, was a winner of ten races, including the 1965 Polish Derby and five other stakes. He sired a few foals in Poland before being exported to Canada. Of his seventy-five purebred offspring, one was a national winner, two were race winners and several competed in recognized endurance rides. Of the endurance horses, four completed California's famed Tevis Cup event, in which horse and rider cover 100 miles in twenty-four hours. All four were bred by the Hyannis Cattle Company of Nebraska, known for its outstanding endurance mounts. Remarkably, one of these four Wosk offspring completed the Tevis ride five times, two of them finished it three times and the one horse that competed in the Tevis ride only once racked up a lifetime total of 4,165 miles in other endurance events.

Gaypolka, imported in utero, was a U.S. National Top Ten Stallion, Canadian Breeders' Champion Stallion and Legion of Merit winner. He sired 125 purebred foals, including a national winner, and was the grandsire of several national winners in a variety of performance disciplines, including cutting, trail, dressage, hunter pleasure, Western pleasure and sidesaddle.

Cypr, which raced unsuccessfully against Orzel in the United States, sired thirty-nine purebred foals, including one national winner. Cypr, like Bajram, is known today as a broodmare sire. His daughters produced numerous performance champions (particularly in the Western disciplines), endurance horses and racehorses. One of Cypr's daughters, Cyroga, was the dam of the well-known stakes winner Magna Terra Smoky, which raced for nine years and amassed winnings of $313,362—an astronomical amount in Arabian racing. A half sister to Magna Terra Smoky, HCC Zaroga, bred by the Hyannis Cattle Company, produced HCC Zarkisia, which racked up 6,455 endurance miles over her thirteen-year career.

Hussar, one of Pietuszok's few foals conceived in Canada, was Regional Top Five Western Pleasure and was also a winner in first-level dressage. Out of eighty-two purebred foals, he sired one national winner and one race winner—the latter going on to become an English pleasure and park champion.

Pietuszok Dwa—*dwa* means "two" in Polish—was so named because of his great resemblance to his sire. Unfortunately, he died in an accident a few weeks before his fifth birthday, having sired only 9 foals. All of these foals, however, bred on. One of them, the stallion Pyatigorsk, which was both a grandson and great-grandson of Pietuszok, sired 338 foals, including national winners, stakes winners and race winners.

Pietuszok's son Pietrak, also foaled in Canada, won three national titles in show hack, Western pleasure and working hunter. He was the sire of forty-two purebred foals, including two national winners.

Pietuszok's last-born son, Black Russian, which was actually gray, sired twenty-four foals, including Mondavai, a regional champion, and race winner Freemark Abbey. As historian Cheryl Hines remarked, "Pietuszok accomplished much in his lifetime, but his impact was only the beginning for what his get and grandget would do. The Russians preferred his brother and the Poles considered him 'common,' but time has proven his record to be one rarely equaled."[74]

Orzel's dam, Ofirka, was foaled at Janow Podlaski Stud in the spring of 1939—a momentous year in world history and a particularly bad time to be born in Poland, which would be ransacked by both Germany and the Soviet Union in short order. In September of that year, when news reached Janow that Germany had overrun Poland, preparations were made to evacuate the horses and head toward the southeast. On September 10, all the stallions were removed from Janow, including Ofirka's sire, Ofir, and her half brother Pamir. The next day, roughly 100 broodmares, 150 young horses (among them Ofirka), numerous handlers and nineteen horse-drawn wagons left the stud.

> *Fearing air raids, they traveled at night, seeking out secondary, unpaved roads in order to preserve the feet of the unshod horses. After the group covered about 40 km (25 miles), it became apparent that they would have to traverse a stretch of paved road…With half the animals already on the paved highway, an impatient driver suddenly switched on his headlights and began to overtake the column. Terrified, four young horses broke away from their handler and galloped off ahead of the vehicle. The sound of their hooves on the pavement, the noise of the truck's engine and the bright lights frightened the other horses…Eighty horses, most of them young, were lost.*[75]

The next morning, the two-year-old colt Taki Pan—later to become Orzel's great-grandsire—was found and returned to the group.

After a few days of relatively trouble-free travel, it began to rain, and

> *as the group approached the town of Kletyck* [now Klityts'k, Ukraine], *the road became exceptionally narrow and muddy and it was bordered on both sides by barbed wire. In the darkness, the riders leading the column could scarcely make out where they were going. Suddenly, one of the lead horses caught its foot on a piece of barbed wire…The animal's terror spread to others in the herd…Horses broke loose and ran in every direction, dragging pieces of fence wrapped around their legs.*

From that incident, three horses had to be humanely destroyed, five were lost and a dozen horses were injured. It was said that Ofirka's sire, Ofir, "had become so entangled in the barbed wire that only his

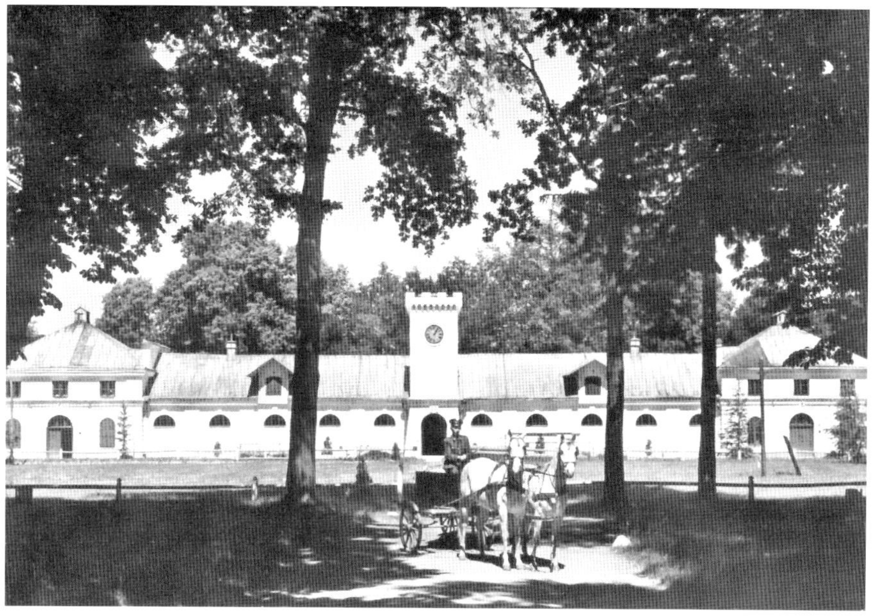

The iconic clock-tower barn at Janow Podlaski State Stud. *Courtesy of Shelley Groom Trevor.*

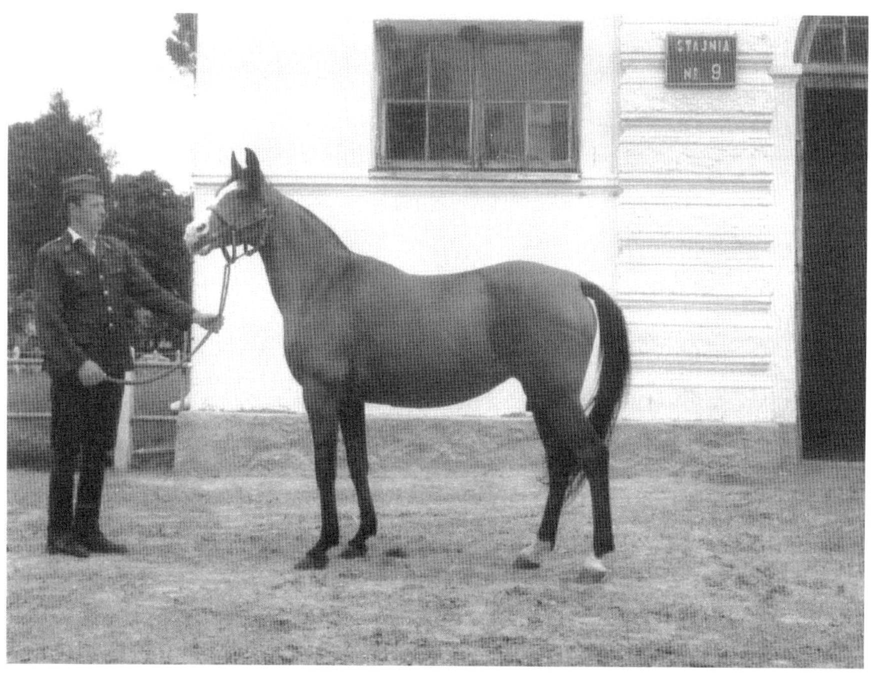

Ofirka, the dam of Orzel, shown here at Janow Podlaski Stud in August 1965, when she was twenty-six years old. *Photograph by and courtesy of Andrew K. Steen.*

extraordinarily calm disposition allowed him to be freed, saving him from certain death."[76]

The group pressed on to the town of Kowel, Volyhnia (now Kovel, Ukraine), where they encountered refugees fleeing Soviet troops moving in from the east. The group's leaders decided then that the best course of action was to return to Janow. "Many horses, mainly foals, perished or had to be left behind at farms or estates along the route, suffering from exhaustion or injury."[77] Fourteen days later, what remained of the herd and its handlers arrived at Soviet-occupied Janow after a fruitless journey of more than two hundred miles. Then, on October 2, "the Soviet regiment enlisted the help of the local population and moved the horses to the eastern side of the Bug River. As it was still without a bridge, the horses were ferried across. It should be noted that these horses taken from Janow were never returned. Most went on to become foundation stock for the Tersk Stud."[78] Among the horses that were confiscated by the USSR were Ofirka's sire, dam and three half sisters, the aforementioned Taki Pan and Piolun—which would become Orzel's grandsire, via Pietuszok. As for Ofirka herself, she was one of the many horses that were lost during that first evacuation. Fortunately, she was found two years later, on a farm in Volyhnia, and returned to Janow. It is said that when the Polish inspector Adam Sosnowski finally found this then-unnamed, malnourished filly, he exclaimed "Ofirka!"—"Ofir's daughter!"—since she so greatly resembled her famous sire, and that epithet became her registered name.[79]

In late October 1939, the Germans retook control of the stud. "Recognizing the worth and importance of Arabian horse breeding, the commanding officer immediately set about rebuilding both facilities and bloodstock… The Germans retained the stud's Polish personnel, including the grooms, and deferred to the Polish experts when it came to breeding."[80] Breeding recommenced in the spring of 1940, and Ofirka's first foal, a chestnut colt named Wernyhora II, was born in 1944. That summer, during the Soviet offensive, the Germans ordered the horses evacuated to southern Saxony, in Germany. By the winter of 1944–45, the horses had been slated to be relocated yet again, this time to Torgau, in northern Saxony—and the route that was chosen went directly through the town of Dresden. On February 13, Janow's eighty stallions were marched into Dresden during the first night of the infamous firebombing by British forces, in which thousands perished. Unaware of what was in store for the city, the colonel in charge of the Janow stallions had *resolved to march straight on with* [the horses] *to the barracks at Dresden. At half-past one they were in the middle of the city, which was under heavy air attack…The stallions went mad and broke loose. In less than a minute there were forty stallions milling around loose, then fifty, then sixty. The men were in almost equal panic…Of eighty stallions, only twenty remained in the morning. Four days were spent in a search for the stragglers, but only thirty-eight could be found, and one of these had already been hitched to a gypsy's wagon. Twenty-two were known to be dead.*

The mares, foals and young stock had spent the night on the road, in the snow and wind, and were driven through the shattered town the next day. "Dr. Andrzej Krzysztalowicz was in charge of the mare party…and as he rode into Dresden, he had to pass the carcasses of his dead stallions lying on the roadside, which almost broke his heart."[81] What was left of Janow's horses made it to Tornau, and thence on to Holstein, where they stayed until the fall of 1946. That year, the horses finally returned to Janow, where the stud began a new chapter in its Arabian breeding program, in which Ofirka would play an important role.

Ofirka was a member of what is arguably the most important female family in Poland—that of Gazella, an Arabian mare imported in 1845 to the breeding farm on the Jarczowce estate of Count Juliusz Dzieduszycki. After the count's death in 1885, his nephew and heir, Count Wojciech Dziedszycki, selected two stallions and twelve mares, including a descendant of Gazella, from his uncle's herd for his Jezupol stud farm. However,

World War I brought a tragic end to the Jarczowce and Jezupol studs. In 1914 the Russian army invaded Count Wojciech Dziedszycki's estate. Every one of his horses was seized and removed from the premises, except for [the mare Pomponia and three fillies, Gazella II, Mlecha and Zulejma]. *These four surviving females…were sent to the Janow Podlaski stud farm, where they were welcomed into its elite broodmare herd. Remarkably, each of the mares established several prolific and influential families—families that are found in some of the most important and successful Polish Arabian horses of today.*[82]

Gazella II, the granddam of Ofirka, was said to be a rather average-looking bay mare, with "an extraordinary ability for adapting to the qualities of each stallion to which she was bred."[83] Her daughters produced the important breeding stallions Ali Said, Lowelas, Opal, Negatiw, Wielki Szlem and

Witraz, as well as many influential broodmares. In the book *Seven Splendids*, Roman Pankiewicz—former deputy director of Poland's Albigowa Stud and keen student of Arabian breeding—discussed seven stallions integral to the Polish breeding program after World War II. Notably, four of the seven were descended from Gazella II: Comet, Negatiw, Wielki Szlem and Witraz.[84]

Ofirka's dam, Fryga II, a bay daughter of the esteemed stallion Bakszysz and Gazella II, was foaled in 1924. Before becoming a broodmare, Fryga II raced for one year, and in four starts, she finished first twice, second once and third once. Fryga II produced a total of ten foals—seven in Poland and three after her forced trek to southwestern Russia. She was the dam of the Oaks winner Ramajana, race winners Onyks and Pamir and four broodmares: Maskota (also a race winner), Nirwana, Ofirka and Wesola. Her two foals born in the USSR, Frina (a full sister to Ofirka) and Konfeta, produced no offspring.

Ofir, sire of Ofirka, was by the desert-bred stallion Kuhailan Haifi and out of Dziwa, a daughter of Zulejma, one of the fillies that accompanied Gazella II to Janow from the estate of Count Wojciech Dziedszycki. A winner of two races, Ofir was known as the best sire in Poland between the two world wars—this despite standing at stud there for only three years, from 1937 to 1939. Lipowicz and Zbyszewski note that Ofir "was not a large horse, but had very refined limbs and an exquisite, dry [refined], expressive head. His greatest merit, however, was that when bred to Janow's mares, his progeny were phenomenal."[85] Indeed, if he had sired only the three stallions Witraz, Wielki Szlem and Witez II, his place in Polish Arabian history would have been ensured. However, he was also an incredible sire of broodmares, such as Mammona, Wierna, Wilga, Wlodarka, Zalotna and, of course, Ofirka.

In the USSR, Ofir's reputation was not nearly so good. For one thing, the Russians preferred rather tall Arabians, and Ofir stood only about 14.2 hands (i.e., five inches shorter than his grandson Orzel). And despite his two wins on the track in Poland, Ofir was considered a "lazy runner" that needed incentive from his jockey's whip—not a trait that Russians cared to perpetuate in their racing-oriented breeding program.[86] As Edwards noted, Ofir "was used at Tersk through 1947, his last foals born in 1948, and of these there were sixteen daughters who became broodmares at Tersk. Only six had daughters which themselves produced any mares kept for breeding. No son, unlike the case in Poland, continued the sire line."[87] However, as time passed, it was clear that the remaining Ofir daughters were producing some high-quality foals. In particular, it was found that crossing the stallion Priboj with daughters or granddaughters of Ofir was a good nick, resulting in such luminaries as the stakes winner and sire Pomeranets and valuable broodmares like Malpia (dam of Muscat), Monopolia (dam of Magnat), Neposeda (dam of Napitok), Pankarta (dam of Podsnejnik), Prowierka (granddam of Prowizja, imported by Ed Tweed) and many others. Orzel himself was bred along these lines (though in Poland, not Russia), since his sire Pietuszok was a top son of Priboj, and of course, Ofirka was a daughter of Ofir.

Pankiewicz has described Ofirka as a small mare (possibly because she was underfed while lost in Volyhnia) that "had a strikingly handsome head and great refinement. Her spectacular Arabian type and golden-bay colour clearly showed the stamp of her sire, the celebrated Ofir. On the 150th anniversary of the Janow Podlaski stud, celebrated in 1967, Ofirka, who was then 28 years old but still full of vigor, represented the pre-war stock of this famous stud."[88]

Between 1944 and 1963, Ofirka produced eighteen foals. Of her fourteen foals that raced, all were winners, and five won stakes races as well, including the Polish Triple Crown winner Orla and the Polish Oaks winner Adis Abeba. Her fourteen racers were by nine sires: Amurath Sahib, El Haifi, Faher, Laur, Marabut, Morocz, Pietuszok, Sedziwoj and Witraz. El Haifi and Witraz belonged to the same sire line as Ofirka—Kuhailan Haifi—while Sedziwoj and Faher were both by Trypolis, and Laur and Pietuszok were both of the Koheilan I sire line.

Orzel is the only son of Ofirka to sire purebred foals; two other sons, Orland and Orszak, were used in siring part-breds. Four daughters of Ofirka were chosen to become broodmares, and three of them established their own breeding dynasties. Ofirka's daughter Gastronomia, foaled in 1946, was described by Pankiewicz as closely resembling "the Arab horses bred in the desert, painted by Juliusz Kossak. She had an exquisite, clean, lean and well set-on head, immense splendid eyes, small, mobile and beautifully chiseled ears. She was big in the girth and had a magnificent set of the tail. Her only shortcoming was her neck: it was not sufficiently long and too thick." Pankiewicz felt that Ofirka's daughter Adis Abeba, born in 1947, was, in terms of type, "closer to her sire [Amurath Sahib] than dam. Of considerable substance, with good conformation and handsome, she was one of the most appreciated brood mares at Michalow [State Stud]." And regarding Orzel's only full sister, Orla, foaled in 1962, he remarked, "She is not only strikingly handsome, full of quality and substance, but also a fine racer: she has captured the Oaks, the Derby and the Weight-for-Age Stakes, twice. She is also notable for transmitting her racing ability to her offspring; her daughter, the chestnut filly Orgia 1971 (by Krczus), has also won the

Oaks, the Derby and the Weight-for-Age."[89] Today, Ofirka—the little filly that was lost for a time in Volyhnia—has descendants throughout the world.

Ofirka delivered Orzel at Janow in 1963, when she was twenty-four years old. He was her last foal—and he had a lot to live up to. Ofirka was not often bred more than once to the same stallion, and it says a great deal about the Poles' high evaluation of her filly Orla that Ofirka was bred again to Pietuszok for her 1963 foal. In contrast to Orla, which was bay like her parents, Orzel was a big chestnut with white legs and an unusual white face marking, including a large, dark spot between his nostril that he inherited from Ofirka (and passed on to some of his own offspring). Unfortunately, there are no descriptions of Orzel as a very young horse. He was born in the same year as several high-quality colts that would, like him, be exported to the United States, including Dar, Emaus, Essaul, Eter, Exelsjor, Flis, Gwar and Zbrucz, his eventual stablemate at Brusally Ranch.

In the fall of 1966, Orzel was put into race training, under the tutelage of Jan Ligocki, a highly experienced conditioner at the Warsaw racetrack. Ligocki had begun his horse career in the 1930s as a groom in the stables of Edward Skorkowski, editor of the Polish Arabian studbook, and became a trainer in 1938.

While there is no specific documentation about Orzel's conditioning regime in Poland, in 1969 Skorkowski wrote an extensive discussion of the training of young Arabians for racing. Presumably, his methods would have been used by Ligocki for Orzel and will be summarized here. In November of their second year, young horses are started under saddle, first at the walk and then the trot. "About a month later, when they have gotten well into their bridles and played with their bits, they begin slowly to canter at first on five furlongs [5/8 of a mile]. The distance is to be lengthened gradually every few weeks so that at the end of the fourth month this slow work reaches about 3 miles of daily canter in two rates of ca. 1½ mile with ten minutes interval in walk." Skorkowski recommended that the trainer should "individualize the work to the possibility of his pupils as well as the atmospheric conditions and training-course quality…A slow canter on a plain, frozen, hard training course doesn't hurt the horses, [it] even hardens the tendons and shoulders." After about four months of this regime, the distance is shortened to about one and a half to two miles, and the pace of the gallop is increased. "In this way, a normal three-year-old Arab approaches the 6 furlongs gallop, and in July on the fifth or fourth day before his debut race, he gets a gallop of 7 furlongs with a canter from 1 mile 2 furlongs."[90] As will be seen, Orzel's first race was in accord with Skorkowski's prescribed schedule, taking place on July 7, 1966.

Before doing a race-by-race analysis of Orzel's Polish starts, it should be noted that Polish records are often rendered in a kind of shorthand. Orzel's record is generally published as 1/7(2-3-1), which means one year of racing, seven starts, two firsts, three seconds, one third place and one finish lower than third place.[91] However, during my research for this book, Tweed's granddaughter Shelley Groom Trevor discovered two different typed copies of Orzel's record. These documents had been furnished to Tweed by Animex, the Polish company that arranged for the colt's sale and export. One document lists six starts, showing that Orzel won two, finished second three times and was third once. The other document shows these six races plus a seventh race, which is listed as an "invalid run." For this race, Orzel's placing is given as "0," and no winning time or money won is provided. Fortunately, I was able to learn the facts behind these two conflicting documents.

I contacted Jakub Kasprzak, of the Polish Jockey Club, in Warsaw to resolve this discrepancy. Kasprzak informed me that the race listed as an "invalid run," which will be detailed below, was indeed annulled by the stewards. This was because *all* of the jockeys had ridden too slowly and thus it was not a fairly contested event. Kasprzak did not know why the jockeys had acted in this way, but he did note that there had been occasions when jockeys "agreed on the results" of a race ahead of time. While it is unclear from extant records at the Jockey Club whether their actions were accidental or calculated, all five jockeys in Orzel's race were penalized. When asked if this race should be counted among Orzel's starts, Kasprzak wrote that Orzel's official record should be "1/7 (2-3-1) but [there] must be information that he started in a race which was annulled."[92] To my knowledge, these facts have never before been published.

Orzel's racing career got off to a splendid start on July 7, 1966, when he won his first race in a time of 1:58. He was ridden by a jockey by the name of Paluszkiewicz, who would ride him in all his starts in Poland. The distance was 1,600 meters (a little less than a mile), and all horses carried 58 kilograms (128 pounds). Orzel defeated four sons of Comet: Admiral (out of Orzel's half sister Adis Abeba), Powoj (out of a full sister to Pietuszok), Flis and Dar. This victory was particularly impressive because Flis and Powoj were co-holders, with Mihrab, of the record for the fastest 1,600-meter races run in 1966.[93] Admiral, which eventually won one stakes race, was later exported to England, where he was used as a breeding stallion. Powoj died sometime between October 1966 and July 1967. Flis and Dar were later exported to the United States, where they both became well-known sires.

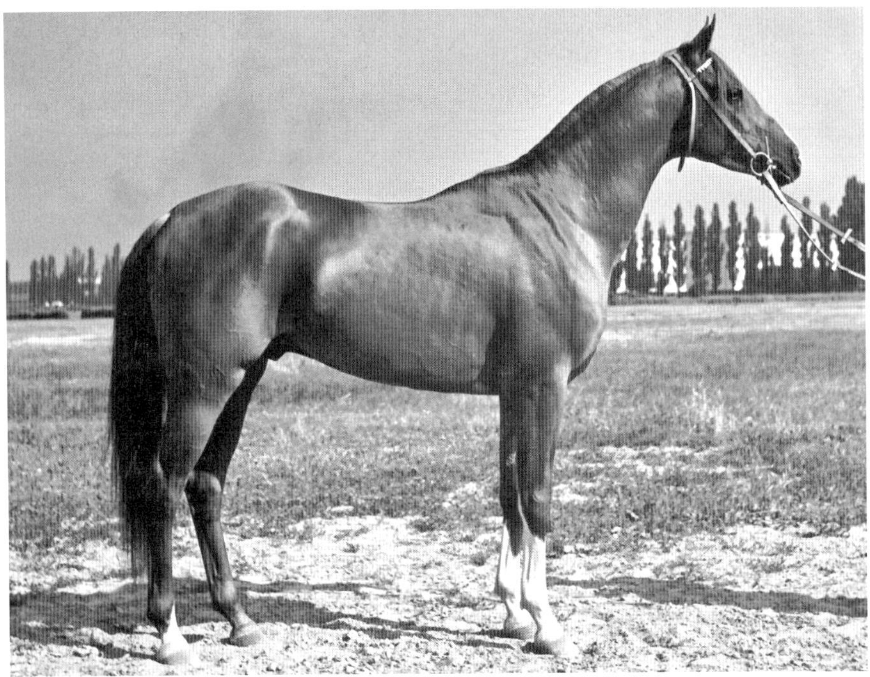

Admiral, a son of Orzel's half sister Adis Abeba, finished behind Orzel in three races in Poland. *Courtesy of Shelley Groom Trevor.*

A little more than a month later, on August 10, Orzel ran in the previously discussed 1,800-meter race that was later annulled because it was run so slowly.[94] The time was 2:13—a full six seconds slower than Orzel's next race at this distance. Orzel finished in third place, behind Admiral and Mihrab, a colt by Pietuszok that was a half brother to Ed Tweed's imported mare Miroluba. Finishing fourth was Cert, another son of Pietuszok, and last was the stakes-winning filly Czartawa. Curiously, this invalid start was the only time in their four races together that Admiral finished in front of Orzel. It was also the first of *only two times* in their five races together that Mihrab came in ahead of Orzel.

Eleven days later, Orzel competed in another 1,800-meter race, placing second behind Krezus, which finished in a time of 2:07—setting a record for the fastest 1,800 meters run in 1966. The winning margin is not known, but one wonders if Orzel goaded Krezus to finish in such a fast time. Behind Orzel came Mihrab, Admiral, Powoj and Cert. All of the horses carried 128 pounds. Krezus would go on to win the Polish Derby, the Criterium and four other stakes. Cert would eventually win three stakes races during his three-year race career.

On September 4, Orzel ran in an 1,800-meter race, finishing third behind Mihrab and Cert and ahead of Flis and Czartawa. Mihrab's time for the distance was 2:08. All horses carried 128 pounds except for Czartawa, which was assigned 124.

Two weeks later, Orzel won his next start, another 1,800-meter race, in a time of 2:10. His paternal half sister Wilma finished second; with Powoj third; Flis fourth; another paternal half sister, Beatrice, fifth; and Admiral last.[95] Wilma would later produce the stakes winner and sire Wiking, and Beatrice would win the Polish Oaks. In this race, the colts carried 128 pounds and the fillies 124.

On October 16, Orzel ran in the Criterium Stakes, at 2,400 meters, against an impressive field, including older horses. He placed second to his talented older sister Orla; she carried 128 pounds while he carried 121. They were followed by the multiple-stakes winner Pien (132 pounds), the race winners Gol and Mihrab (both 132 pounds) and Wosk, the previous year's Polish Derby winner (141 pounds). The winning time was 2:55, one second faster than Orla's winning time in this race the previous year. Notably, Orla, Orzel, Mihrab and Wosk were all offspring of Pietuszok.

Orzel's last race in Poland, the Amurath Stakes, at 2,200 meters, took place on October 30. All of the starters carried approximately 128 pounds. The winner was Krezus, in a time of 2:43, followed by Orzel, Mihrab, Cert and Powoj. Of these five colts, only two—Orzel and Krezus—would go on to sire offspring. Among Krezus's many talented foals, his daughter Orgia—out of Orzel's sister, the speedy Orla—was a winner of the Polish Triple Crown.

In 1988, Edwards recalled:

> *When we were in Poland that first time, Mr. Poniatowski (of Animex) kept referring to a horse which had just been sold to America, which he explained meant "eagle" or "hawk"—take your pick. He spoke so highly of this colt and his famous sister, Orla, that it was difficult not to get jealous of the lucky person who acquired him, namely Ed Tweed…This dark red chestnut was a powerfully built horse, with a beautiful slope and length of shoulder, and although his croup was not dead level, it was* long. *As might be expected, he had ample bone.*[96]

After his importation to the United States in the spring of 1967, Orzel was put into race training at Brusally Ranch. It took a while for the colt to settle into his new routine and adjust to American methods, including

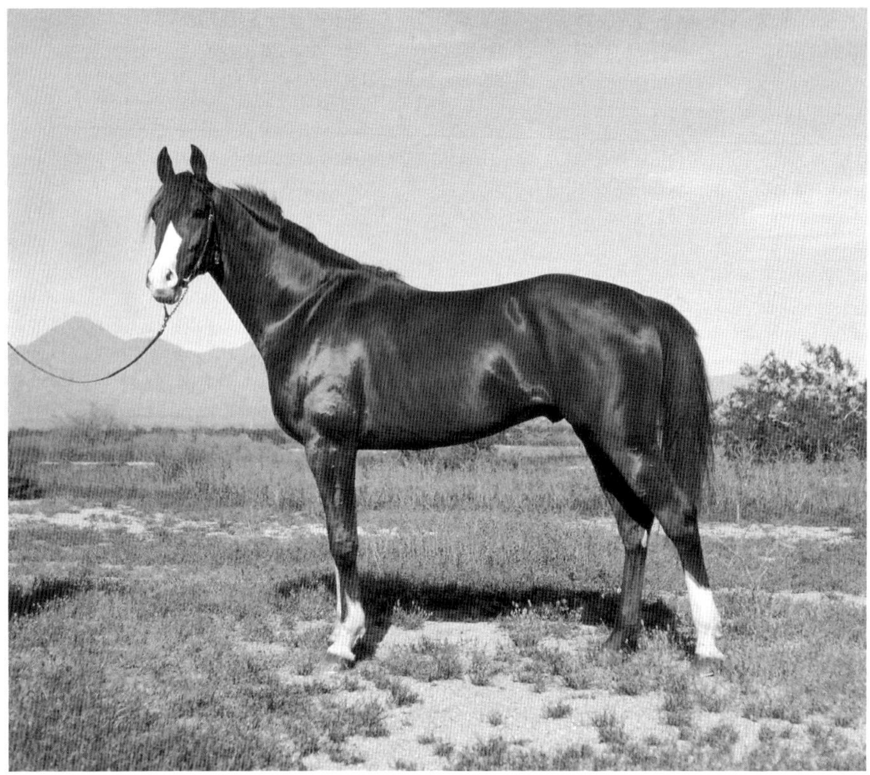

Orzel at Brusally Ranch, soon after his 1967 importation from Poland. *Photo by Nancy Reidhead, courtesy of Shelley Groom Trevor.*

running on a dirt track—all of his starts in Poland had been on the turf. Trevor remembered "the crew struggling to saddle him in the paddock stall. The big horse was alternately trying to lie down or rear."[97] And Tweed noted that while "the training [Orzel] received in Warsaw was of some help to him…when he arrived here, he was very much in need of training in this country, which we proceeded to have done at considerable expense before we could put him on the track."[98]

In the United States, Orzel first competed in two races that are not part of his official U.S. race record. In August 1967, three races were run at the New Mexico State Fairgrounds in Albuquerque, in conjunction with the U.S. National Championship Show. Eight horses, including Orzel, trained by Denis Scully, were entered in the International Arabian Horse Association Show Racing Derby, which was held on August 13. The race was apparently a rather amateurish affair; the horses were ridden by both jockeys and nonprofessional riders, and the method of starting the race consisted of leading the horses onto the track, and then "the eight racers were turned over to the starter…After a brief warm-up the horses were walked in front of the grandstand. As they neared the mile point, [the starter] got them all pointed in the same direction and in a reasonably straight line, and then they were off!" The one-mile race was won by Lilly Eda Ku in a time of 2:04 4/5, which was more than twelve seconds slower than Orzel would run in an exhibition race, ridden by a professional jockey, a few weeks later. The complete order of finish for this derby is unclear, but suffice it to say that Orzel was not among the top five finishers.[99] (Interestingly, Tweed's imported racing mare Cerera, which had won three races in Poland, ran in the first race of this three-day meet—which was held in the driving rain—and she, too, finished near the back of the pack.) This defeat taught Tweed a valuable lesson about Orzel's preferred way of running: the colt strongly objected to the jockey's use of the whip. As Trevor recalled, "Later, as a halter horse, too, Orzel would pull into himself at the lash of a whip, as if to curb his spirit and be obedient instead. He could be inspired but not forced."[100]

After his disappointing run in New Mexico, Orzel was then shipped to Evangeline Downs in Lafayette, Louisiana. Although Arabians had raced sporadically in the United States since 1959, when the first exhibition race was held at Laurel Park in Maryland, the September 1967 meet would be the first time that Arabians had raced under parimutuel conditions, the system used in Thoroughbred racing.[101] Because none of the Arabians running at Evangeline Downs had official race records by which the track's handicappers could grade and assess them, the track officials stipulated that before the meet began, three unofficial exhibition races—at one mile, one and a quarter miles and one and a half miles—would be held. On August 24, Orzel, now trained by Thoroughbred conditioner Paul Pellerin and ridden by professional jockey James F. Young, competed in the one-mile race. The win photo shows that Orzel triumphed by at least six lengths over the aged Al-Marah Ibn Indraff, which finished so far back that he did not appear in the picture. Arwallany was third.

Orzel resumed his official racing career on September 4, ten months after his last start in Poland. His first American parimutuel race, the Invitational Handicap, was run at the unusual distance of one mile, four and a half furlongs—longer than any of his races in Poland. Carrying 116 pounds and again piloted by Young, Orzel covered the distance in 3:04 4/5, defeating Ibn Saka by a neck. Commissar was third, and Cypr, Orzel's paternal half brother, was fourth.

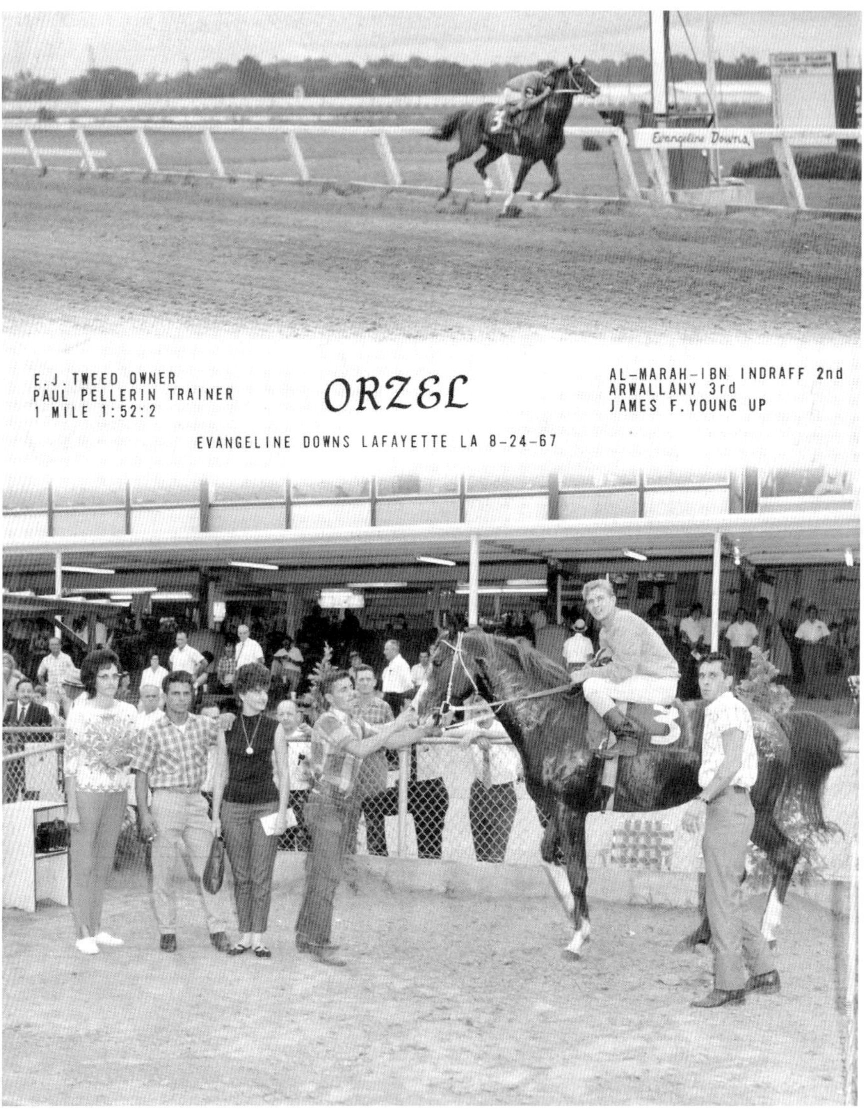

Orzel won an unofficial exhibition race on August 24, 1967, days prior to the start of
the first parimutuel race meet for Arabians at Evangeline Downs in Lafayette, Louisiana.
Courtesy of Shelley Groom Trevor.

Five days later, competing in the Open Handicap at Evangeline Downs
at the same distance, with Young in the irons, Orzel carried two more
pounds and led from wire to wire, shaving more than four seconds off his
previous performance. Two lengths behind Orzel came Ibn Saka, followed

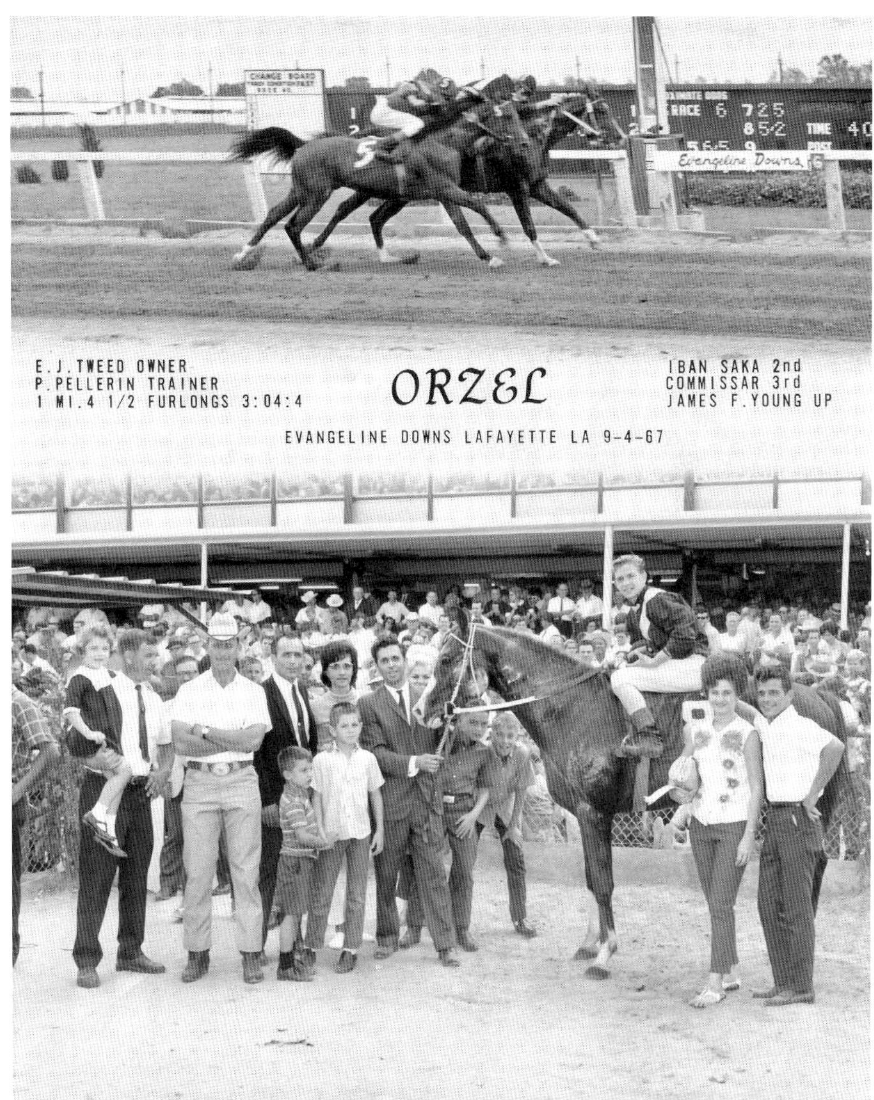

Orzel finished first over Ibn Saka at Evangeline Downs in Lafayette, Louisiana, on September 4, 1967. *Courtesy of Shelley Groom Trevor.*

by El Gohari. Cypr was again fourth. For this victory, Orzel was awarded the Evangeline Downs Arabian Championship, making him the 1967 U.S. National Champion Racehorse, the first to be so honored.

After a hiatus of more than two months, Orzel's next racing appearance took place much closer to his home turf—Turf Paradise, that is, in Phoenix,

Arizona. This, too, was a parimutuel meet featuring sixty Arabians that ran from November 1967 to March 1968. On November 19, eight horses went to the post for the first Arabian race held in Arizona. The one-and-a-half-mile race turned into a battle between Orzel, shouldering 130 pounds and ridden by a new jockey, G. Cavalier, and El Gohari, which had finished third in their last meeting and now carried 128 pounds. The official chart for the race read, "El Gohari saved ground early, opened a clear lead before a mile and was kept under pressure through the stretch. Orzel went up on the outside to be nearest the leader on the backstretch but could not close the gap."[102] Orzel was beaten by two lengths, with Al-Marah Indraff third and Rajilita Ku fourth.[103] This was not the Arizona debut that Tweed had wanted his chestnut champion to make, and one wonders what the outcome would have been if Orzel had been ridden again by Young. However, as an observer noted, "This first race at Phoenix was a crowd pleaser and the officials of the track were happy with the handle [amount of money wagered], and the racing commissioners were not unhappy with the race because of the strong showing of the first two horses."[104]

Orzel's first race of 1968 took place on February 25, when he faced eight opponents in another one-and-a-half-mile race at Turf Paradise. This time, he carried 140 pounds, 10 more than in his previous race, and had another new jockey, the experienced Frank Inda, whose successful racing career took him to the Pacific Northwest, where he was a champion rider. In this outing, Orzel, now trained by Denis Scully, was co-high weight with Ibn Saka, which he had defeated twice in Louisiana. However, Ibn Saka had himself won a one-and-a-half-mile race during the Turf Paradise meeting, as had some of Orzel's other rivals in this race, including Kemas Polka (which carried 130 pounds) and Silki (114 pounds). The official chart for the race read, "Orzel went up on outside to draw clear before a mile, raced nearest rail and was never seriously threatened. Ibn Saka moved strongly when urged on far turn but could not close gap. Ibn Shara led for nearly a mile but gave way gradually."[105] Orzel won by six lengths over Ibn Saka, with Ibn Shara third.

In late March, Orzel was back at Turf Paradise, where he was again conditioned by Pellerin. Carrying yet another new rider, Dick Culbertson, as well as high weight of 142 pounds, Orzel would face the most accomplished field of his American race career, including the winners Ibn Saka, Kemahs Polka, Ben Hib Ku, Ibn Shara, Nusabre, Silki and Ghami—the latter carrying only 106 pounds. However, Orzel's only real competition was the white-gray phenomenon Kontiki, unbeaten in his first three races, all at Turf Paradise. On December 20, Kontiki had gotten his racing career off to an impressive start: carrying 119 pounds, he had faced eight other horses, beating the second-place finisher, Cypr, by twenty lengths. About three weeks later, Kontiki won by seven lengths over Al-Marah Ibn Indraff, and two weeks after that, with an impost of 140 pounds, he again defeated Cypr, this time by three lengths but spotting him 21 pounds. Now, just as he

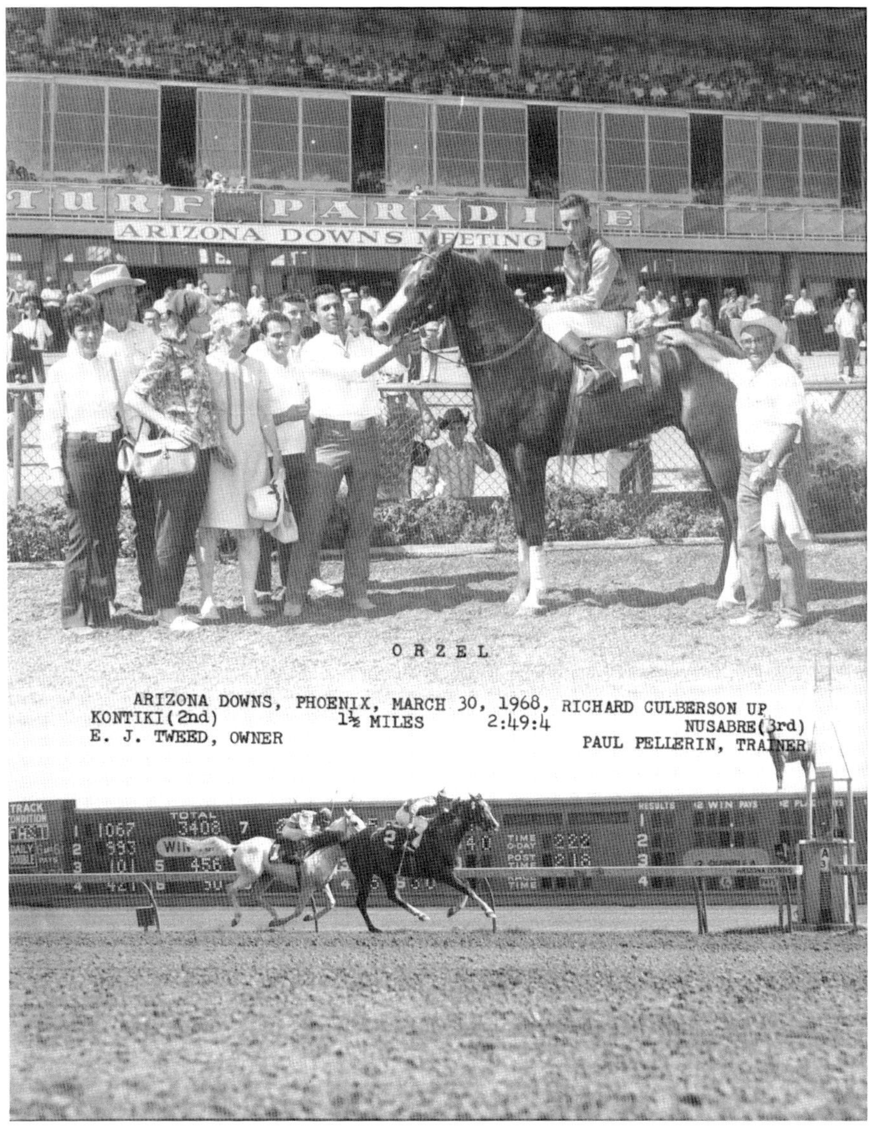

Carrying 142 pounds to his rival's 140, Orzel defeated the great Kontiki at Turf Paradise in Phoenix, Arizona, on March 30, 1968. *Courtesy of Shelley Groom Trevor.*

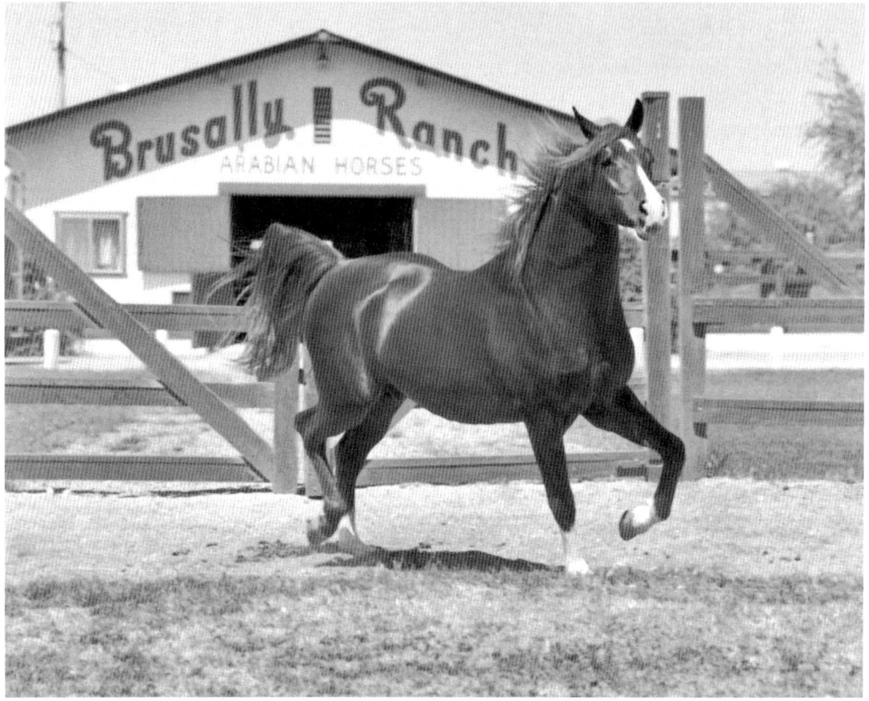

After his retirement from racing, Orzel returned to Brusally Ranch, where he began his training as a show horse. *Courtesy of Shelley Groom Trevor.*

had in his previous races, Kontiki was ridden by veteran jockey Bob Yeager and again carried 140 pounds. Fans knew they would be watching a real match race—like Seabiscuit versus War Admiral—and made Kontiki the slight betting favorite since he had won so convincingly in his earlier races and was carrying 2 fewer pounds than Orzel. However, the official chart for this one-and-a-half-mile race noted, "Orzel, permitted to race far off early pace, went up on outside when gaining steadily on backstretch and was hard ridden when drawing clear entering stretch. Kontiki, reserved when leading to upper stretch, continued gamely but could not manage winner. Nusabre forced leader in early going but weakened in stretch run."[106] Finally, Kontiki had met his match. Edwards remarked, "The hardest-fought race of all was the ding-dong battle between Orzel and Kontiki, with the former winning over the previously unbeaten Kontiki."[107] This race would be Kontiki's sole defeat in his nine-race career. It was also to be Orzel's last start, though Tweed did not know that yet.

Tweed had expected to race Orzel again in a few weeks at Turf Paradise—where he would have faced Kontiki and El Gohari in another one-and-a-half-mile race—and then prepare him for the fall meet at Evangeline Downs. In a turn of events that resembled Samuel Riddle's decision to retire the great Man O'War, the Turf Paradise handicapper informed Tweed that in his next race, Orzel would be expected to carry an unprecedented 146 pounds. Although Orzel came out of his race against Kontiki completely sound, Tweed heeded the advice of racetrack veterinarians—who warned against running Orzel under such an impost—and took his chestnut champion back to Brusally Ranch. There, Orzel would begin training for the second act of his performance career: as a show horse.

Chapter 5

THE HORSE OF A LIFETIME

Orzel and his stablemate Zbrucz were not the only new arrivals at Brusally Ranch in 1967. That spring, Ed and Ruth Tweed invited three of their young granddaughters—Bruce's daughters, Bonnie and Susie Tweed, and Sally's daughter, Shelley Groom (later Trevor)—to visit them in Scottsdale with the idea that perhaps one of the girls would be interested in staying on and learning about horses and horsemanship. Ruth noted that the three girls "were darling and didn't ask for anything more than just to play around the stable and to love and ride the horses. Bonnie and Sue know practically nothing about riding, but Shelley is an excellent rider. Denis Scully took one look at her on [the Polish stallions] Faraon and Czester and right away propositioned us about getting her out here this summer to go to the shows…Shelley was so thrilled that she could hardly bring herself to go back to finish her year at the university."[108] Trevor herself recalled, "When you fall in love, you don't have to ask, 'Shall I?' You know. And when my grandfather posed the question, 'Would one of you want to come to live and work permanently at Brusally?' I was the only one who saw stars." At age twenty-one, Trevor "fell in love with a ranch. Brusally was the place I'd love, work, and call home for 17 years."[109]

Trevor was born in 1945 in Chicago as Chaille Anne Groom and was reared in Charleston, South Carolina. She began riding at age six, when her mother won a pinto pony, complete with saddle and bridle, from a local grocery store. The pony, named Johnny Rebel, was aptly named, as he regularly attempted to get rid of his rider, whether by running under low-hanging tree limbs or through Dutch doors. As she grew older, Trevor rode other equines that her family acquired. She spent many years riding bareback in the South Carolina Lowcountry, keeping an eye out for potentially dangerous pluff mud—a local term denoting what one writer called "an oozy, viscous, dark-brown miasma…You can't really call yourself a Charlestonian until you have sacrificed a shoe or two to its gooey, vise-like clutch."[110]

By the time she was eleven, Trevor was hungry to learn more about horses, writing:

> *I was up at six to follow a friend of the family's, Pete, a horse breeder, down to a local hotel where we joined company with trainers and had breakfast. From there the day was a round of stables, show grounds and auctions. They called me "Pete's Shadow." All day I watched horses as these men did, as men always have—as if nothing could be of greater interest than a leg, a hoof, a pedigree. Sometimes, it was later said, I would be found sleeping on a bale of straw. But I had the thrill of riding a World's Champion* [Tennessee Walking Horse] *and was given a retired show horse. This hunger to observe horses and to ride them was never to change.*[111]

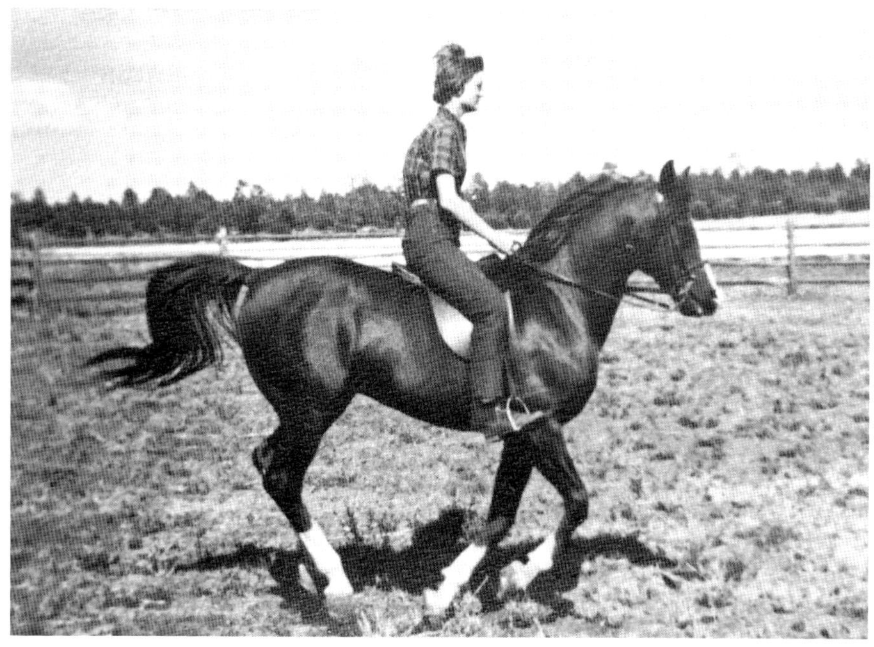

Trevor riding Skorage at the Tweeds' ranch near Show Low, Arizona, in 1961. *Courtesy of Shelley Groom Trevor.*

The World's Champion to which she referred was Go Boy's Shadow, a handsome black stallion owned by Winston Wiser and E.H. Padgett that in 1955 was named both the Junior Walking Horse Champion of the World and the Grand Champion Walking Horse of the World. Many years later, a Tennessee Walking Horse aficionado in Arizona told Trevor how impressed he was that she had "thrown a leg over" Go Boy's Shadow. But Shadow was merely the first of many well-known horses that Trevor would ride.

In fact, years before Ed and Ruth concocted the idea to have one of their granddaughters work at Brusally, Trevor had visited them at their northern Arizona ranch, nestled among the Ponderosa pines of the White Mountains. There, in 1961, she had the opportunity to ride her first Arabian—Skorage—and the pair even accompanied Brusally's string of show horses to Estes Park, Colorado, where the U.S. National Championships were held that year. Trevor showed Skorage in an amateur English pleasure class, saying later, "I didn't know much, but he was a push-button horse, and he knew his job. We won second place easily." Regarding Skorage's personality, she found him to be "charismatic" and "a true professional. His disposition couldn't have been better; he was easy to handle, a true gentleman."[112]

Trevor recalled that

> *as a teenager, I rode any horse I could, which included a high-stepping, roman-nosed, bay Hackney pony. We would jump anything, even a single chair in an open field. I jumped in and out of the ring, rather than go through the gate. At a show in Tryon, North Carolina, we cleared the last fence at 5' 2" in a class called "six bars" (six in-and-out hurdles). I just wove my fingers into his mane, gave him lots of rein, perched forward, and let him go. The brave pony sprang over the tall fences, one after the other, in perfect rhythm. When the last fence was raised to 5'4", he tried his best but the top poles fell. We came home with a second-place ribbon. I knew next to nothing about jumping technique. Having complete trust in Tipperary Tim's ability, I never considered the fact that the other exhibitors were professionals on lanky Thoroughbreds.[113]*

By the time Trevor relocated to Scottsdale in late 1967, she had completed two years of study at Stephens College, an all-female institution in Columbia, Missouri, that had a nationally renowned equestrian program and then studied fine art for a year at the University of Colorado, Boulder. She later transferred to Arizona State University in Tempe, from which she would graduate with a bachelor's degree in art. Like her grandfather, Trevor was athletic and artistic; she had initially considered teaching art but quickly discarded that career path when she realized she had the opportunity to become a professional equestrian. However, she had a number of hurdles to overcome.

Although outsiders assumed that being the boss's granddaughter was a sure way to success—as one local reporter quipped, "What young rider would not give her silver stirrups to be in [Trevor's] shoes?"—her first year at Brusally consisted of mucking stalls, sweeping the barn aisles, grooming show horses, walking racehorses after their workouts and only rarely getting the opportunity to ride.[114] Over time, though, she moved up from her position as a groom, becoming a competitor, a trainer and, finally, the ranch manager. "Many days," she noted, "the best I could do was put one foot in front of the other, keep working, keep trying. Today, I believe that had the initial infatuation not been so intense, I would not have had the commitment to endure these trials."[115]

One person who helped Trevor on her journey was Kay Braswell, a local riding teacher with a varied equestrian background, including training polo ponies in west Texas; showing at Stephens College, where she also taught saddleseat and huntseat equitation; and riding lead ponies at Rillito Park Racetrack in Tucson. By 1968, when Trevor began training with Braswell, her instructor had been confined to a wheelchair for two decades after a bout of polio. Braswell, a gifted teacher, took "a vicarious pleasure in seeing others ride and participate in shows."[116] Trevor recalled that, for months, "I worked with her from 8 to noon, 5 days a week…Kay taught me to post from the balls of my feet, up and down with the trot, balanced, like floating, which created a style unlike most riders of the day."[117] Braswell also introduced Trevor to riding sidesaddle, a discipline in which she would later earn two national titles, on Orzel and his son Mohawk Chief.

In 1968, Trevor made her Arabian horse showing debut at the annual Arabian show in Santa Barbara. Years later, the trauma of that first show was still evident, as Trevor recalled driving Skorzah, a daughter of Skorage, in a pleasure class: "As horses and buggies blazed into the arena, I was locked in a petrified world, not connected with the powerfully trotting mare before me. Alienated in an intense environment of about twenty fast-moving horses, she bolted and then spun into the ring's center, throwing me from the four-wheeled buggy to land almost at the judge's feet." In her torn stockings and ruined pink dress, Trevor picked herself up and trudged toward the arena's exit gate. There she was met by a familiar face, Dr. Eugene LaCroix of Scottsdale's Lasma Arabians, who kindly inquired whether she was all right. Nodding mutely, she escaped to the solace of a quiet tack room, where she spent the afternoon crying:

> *After I emotionally recovered (not an easy task!), with nothing more to lose—I couldn't do worse—I was free. Skorzah and I were free to be the team we could be. At the ranch, I'd known we had something special. I'd felt the mare's swift power and my ability to float with her energy. The next day, we sped around that arena of fifty-one fancy horses, and won. Over the years, through failure and success, horses made me the rider and person that I am.*[118]

The following February, Trevor campaigned three mares at the Scottsdale Show, gaining more valuable show experience and winning a few classes. She showed Brusally Faronifa in English and Western pleasure; Ed-Mar Michelle in formal combination, formal driving and park; and Skorzah in English pleasure, native costume, pleasure driving and sidesaddle (all uneventfully, this time). Later in the year, after months of showing, Trevor won her first national title—U.S. National Top Ten Formal Driving, with Ed-Mar Michelle—at the 1969 U.S. National Championship show.

While Trevor was learning to show Arabians, Orzel was transitioning from his previous life as a highly animated, forward-thinking racehorse to a new career as a halter horse, where he learned to stand at attention for minutes at a time while the judges examined him from various angles. At the 1969 Las Vegas Arabian Horse Show, judged by Charley Araujo and Robert L. Armstrong, Orzel was named champion stallion, with Sur Fad the reserve champion. In the halter class for his age group, Orzel was awarded first place over twenty-three other stallions, including Tazyk, Phazon, Talal and Dokhailan.

At the Arabian Horse Association of Southern California Horse Show in Santa Barbara, judged by Al Mecham and Robert L. Whitney, Orzel bounded into the show ring led by Brusally's manager/trainer Charlie Carter. "A powerhouse of race-track energy, his lean, muscular form now filled out, he literally took people's breath away," Trevor recalled. "They couldn't take their eyes off this magnificent red 'stranger.'"[119] As Orzel reared and played, Carter simply let him be himself—and the crowd loved it. Orzel won the stallions six and over class, defeating Sur-Elite, Royal Binis, Farolito, Green Acres Zeus and five others, and then was named champion stallion—over a charismatic youngster named Khemosabi. This legendary bay stallion would go on to win multiple

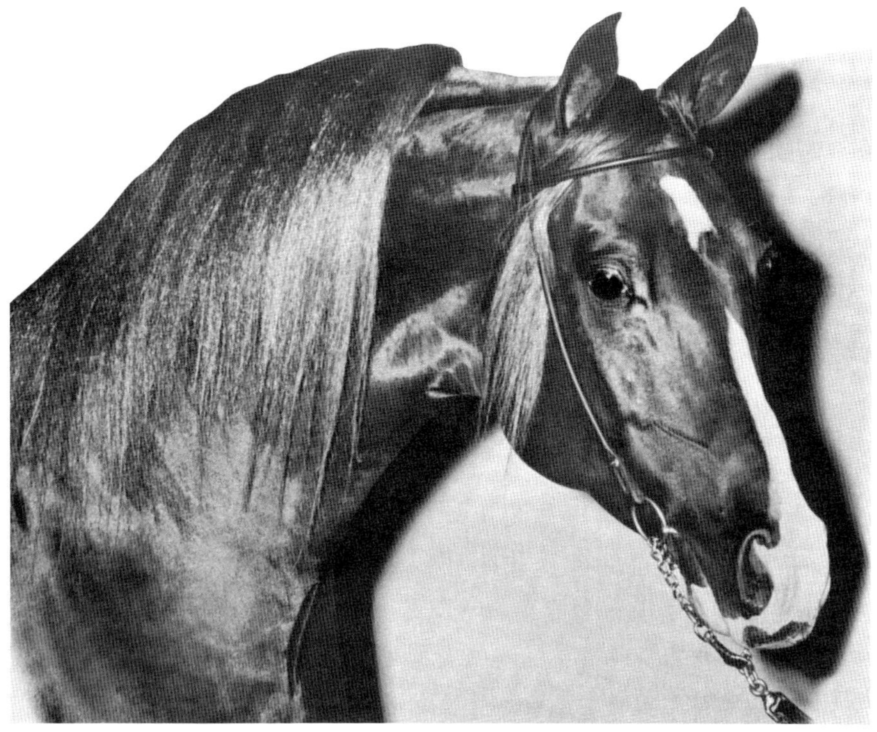

Orzel competing in a halter class. *Courtesy of Shelley Groom Trevor.*

national championships, sire more than 1,200 foals and be immortalized as a Breyer model horse.

At the 1969 U.S. National Championship Show, held in Oklahoma City and judged by Byron H. Good, James J. Kiser and Donald M. Wardle, Orzel competed against sixty-five of the country's best stallions in the halter championship. Galizon was named U.S. National Champion Stallion, Gwalior was U.S. Reserve National Champion Stallion and Orzel was named a U.S. National Top Ten Stallion, along with Ansata Ibn Halima, Ansata Ibn Sudan, El Raffon, Farolito, Serj, Talal and Tazyk. Tweed was mightily pleased with his racehorse turned show horse's record in his first year of showing, and he looked forward to seeing what the big red horse would do the following year.

Orzel's 1970 debut was at Tweed's beloved Scottsdale Show, judged by Lee Caldwell, Mrs. Harold A. Gardiner and Byron H. Good. Orzel was named the winner of his age class, over the well-known Aramus (owned by entertainer Wayne Newton), Talal, Green Acres Galaxy, Mr. Storm and sixteen others. The judges then crowned Orzel the champion stallion, with Counselor the reserve

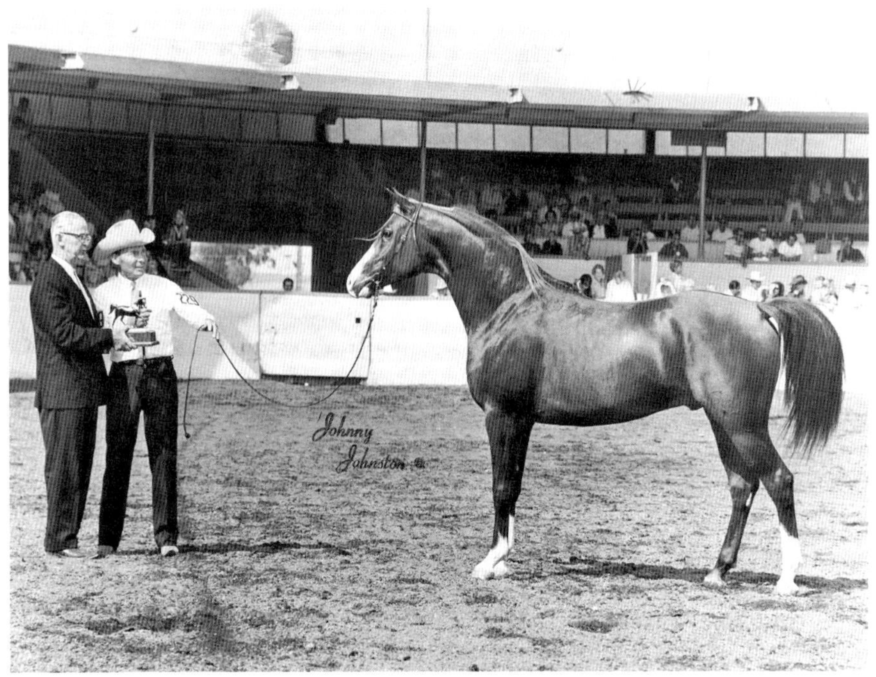

Charlie Carter showed Orzel when he won the stallion championship at the 1969 Arabian Horse Association of Southern California Horse Show in Santa Barbara, California. *Photo by Johnny Johnston, courtesy of Shelley Groom Trevor.*

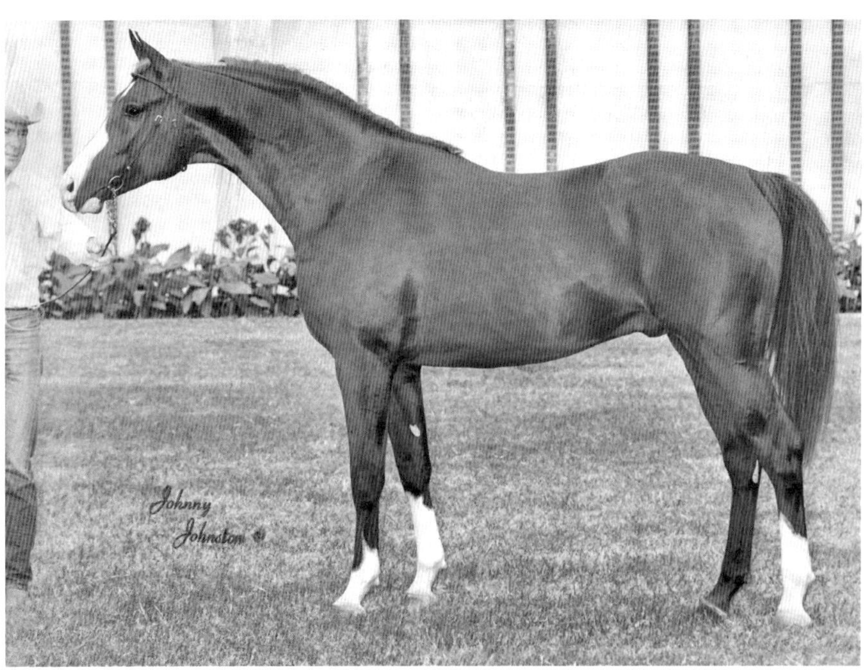

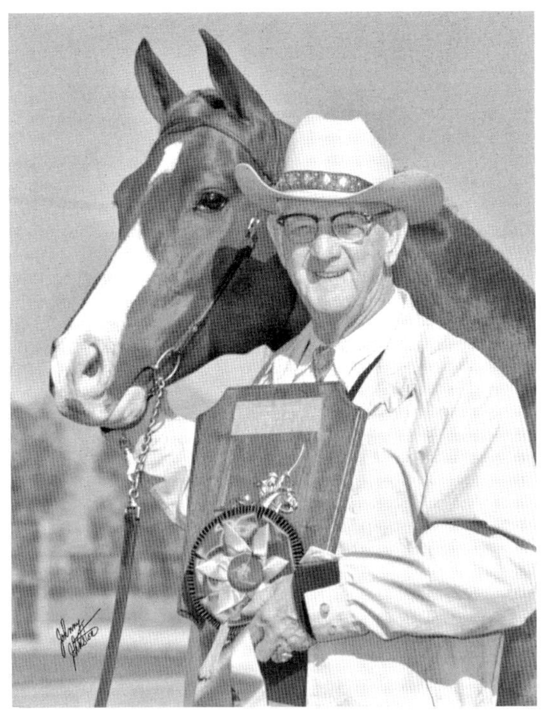

Right: Tweed was overjoyed when Orzel won the stallion championship at the Scottsdale Show in 1970. *Photograph by Johnny Johnston, courtesy of Shelley Groom Trevor.*

Below: Brusally Orzelyna, a filly from Orzel's first crop, won the yearling filly class at a 1970 show in Tucson, Arizona. *Photo by Johnny Johnston, courtesy of Shelley Groom Trevor.*

Opposite, bottom: Charlie Carter and Orzel at the 1969 U.S. National Championship Arabian Horse Show in Oklahoma City. *Photo by Johnny Johnston, courtesy of Shelley Groom Trevor.*

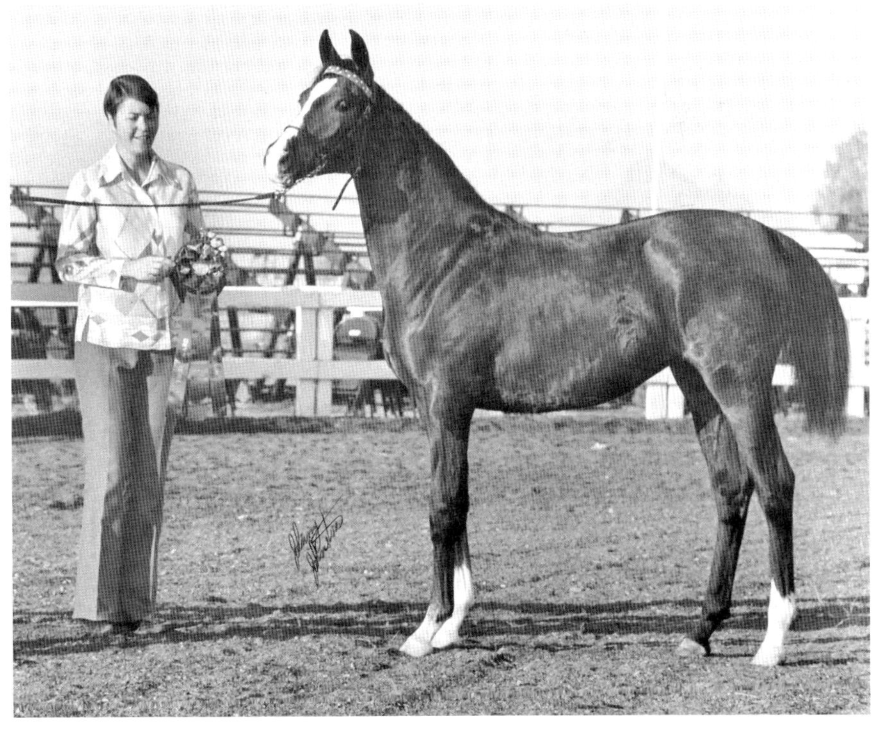

champion. To add to Tweed's delight, the lovely gray Brusally Orzelyna, a foal from Orzel's first crop, won the large yearling fillies class.

Orzel's next victory came at the Kansas All-Arabian Horse Show in Salina, judged by James J. Kiser and Victor E. Oppegard. In the first round of competition, Orzel faced twenty-one stallions over four years of age, winning the class. Grand Lee, Serrik, Rolo Baytila and Kaw Liga were among the top five finishers. Orzel was named champion stallion over Grand Lee.

Then it was on to the Arabian Horse Club of Texas's Annual Arabian Horse Show, held in Dallas, where Orzel was named both senior champion stallion and show champion stallion over Beau Ibn Hanrah, judged by Cotton Marriott, Victor E. Oppegard and H. Karl Yenser. In addition to Beau Ibn Hanrah, the other top finishers in Orzel's age class included Ramaraas of Delta C, Halin and Surmyn.

Orzel qualified for the U.S. National Championship Show again in 1970, when, shown by Hank Ack, he was selected as one of twenty stallions, out of sixty-four, to proceed to the Top Ten. However, he was not chosen for the final lineup of Top Ten Stallions, which included El Raffon and Farolito, horses he had previously defeated. That year, Aramus—another horse that had been shown against Orzel and lost—was named U.S. National Champion Stallion, and Gwalior was again U.S. Reserve National Champion. The judges were E.J. Fairbanks, W. Lyman Orcutt and Cecil F. Rooks.

The year 1971 was a bittersweet time for Ed Tweed; although his horses were winning championships nationwide, and his granddaughter was seeing much success in the show ring, his wife of fifty-four years, Ruth, passed away after a long illness in February, just days after the Scottsdale Show. Still, somehow, Ed carried on, though he began to turn over more of the ranch's day-to-day affairs to Trevor.

That spring, Tweed sent Orzel to Ogden, Utah, where he was named champion stallion at the Golden Spike All Arabian Horse Show, judged by James J. Kiser. The chestnut stallion faced eight horses in his age class, including Rampage, Seyadan, Fixseyn and Pierrekameyn. Reserve champion to Orzel was Cougar, which had won the four-year-old stallion class.

At the Region 5 Arabian Show held at the State Fair of Texas in Dallas, judged by Al Mecham, Orzel was named a Top Five Stallion. Regional Champion Stallion was Sakr, and Reserve Regional Champion was Faleh, with Wiraz and Don Amistad rounding out the Top Five.

The 1971 Canadian National Championship Show in Edmonton, Alberta, was judged by Peter Cameron, Byron H. Good and Victor E. Oppegard. Orzel received the title of Canadian National Top Ten Stallion, along with two horses he had previously defeated, Counselor and Khemosabi. Gwalior was named Canadian National Champion Stallion, while Eleuzis claimed the title of Canadian Reserve National Champion.

Tweed now owned the first horse to be named U.S. National Champion Racehorse, U.S. National Top Ten Stallion and Canadian National Top Ten Stallion. However, there would be many more accolades to come before Orzel's show career came to a close.

In 1972, Trevor began showing Orzel under saddle: "At first, riding a horse who'd just as soon be airborne as not was intimidating. But he quickly proved himself to be as much a gentleman and a lady's mount as he was a track star."[120] In addition to being crowned the champion stallion at the Comstock All Arabian Horse Show in Reno, Nevada, Orzel won the show's English pleasure championship, judged by Ralph E. Hager and Gladys Wikoff. A few weeks earlier, Orzel had also been named champion stallion at the Las Vegas All Arabian Horse Show, judged by Harold Brite and Helen Ittner.

At San Francisco's Grand National Horse Show, held at the famed Cow Palace, judge Robert L. Whitney chose Orzel as the winner of the thirty-seven-horse open English pleasure class and later named him the Pacific

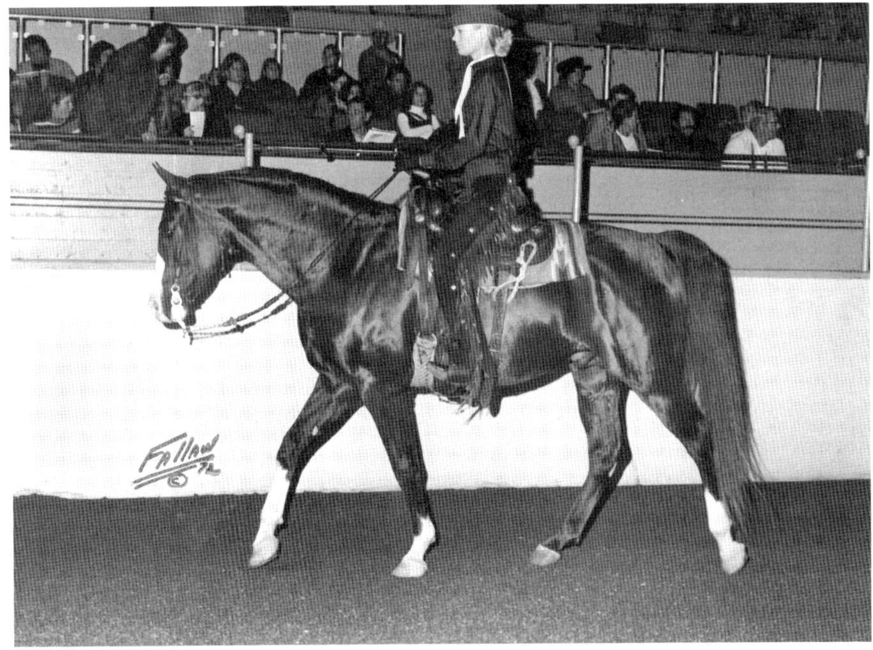

Orzel competing in Western pleasure with Trevor astride. *Photo by June Fallaw, courtesy of Shelley Groom Trevor.*

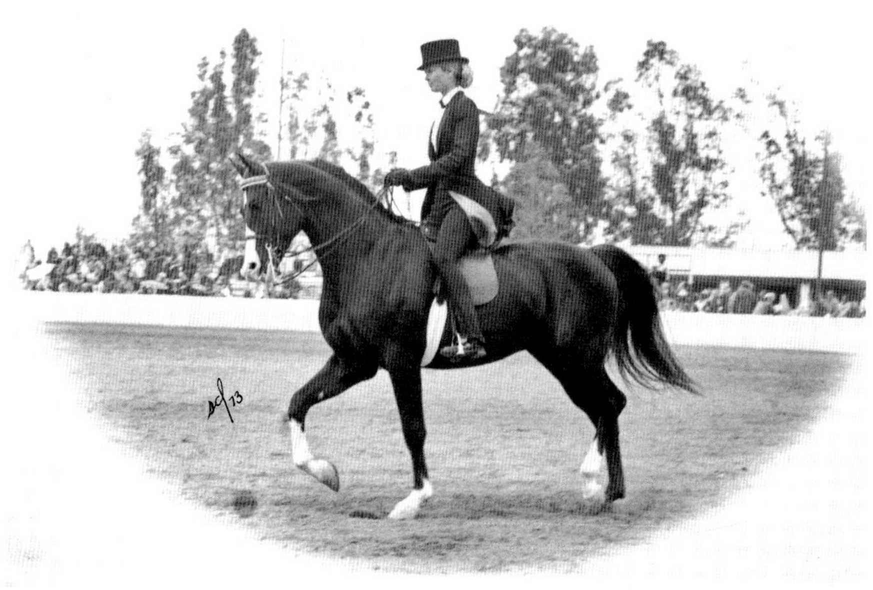

Trevor riding Orzel in an English pleasure class. *Courtesy of Shelley Groom Trevor.*

Slope English pleasure champion over thirty-two rivals. Orzel also won the sidesaddle class. "As I rode him on the show grounds to the arena," wrote Trevor, "heads would turn. He didn't need to be animated, jazzed into a nervy show horse 'presence' to stand out from the crowd. Orzel was just himself, a big red king, with clean limbs and a calm, intelligent nature."[121]

Because of Orzel's record as a racehorse and show horse, he was named a "Proud Performer" by the International Arabian Horse Association, and Trevor was invited to exhibit him each evening at the 1972 U.S. National Championship Show in Oklahoma City. Wearing jockey's silks and riding Orzel in a racing saddle, Trevor galloped around the darkened arena, her path lit only by a spotlight. One evening, after her nightly ride, she was approached by a man who had been awestruck by the big red stallion and his blond jockey. That spectator was Walter Farley, author of *The Black Stallion, The Island Stallion, Man O' War* and other books beloved by children and adults alike. This meeting marked the beginning of a friendship that would last until the end of Farley's life in 1989.

In a letter to Tweed, Farley wrote about his excitement at seeing Orzel:

Long ago I remember friends in the East, returning from Western trips and telling of the new, different, beautiful Arabians (Polish Arabians) they had seen. And it filled me with joy because my Black Stallion was "ahead of his time" and Brusally (Ed and Ruth Tweed) were importing and breeding/raising such horses. Therefore, I was justified in making my Black Stallion what he was to the eye—big and fast but with all the beauty of an Arabian…if you take Orzel, paint him black, add a little height and speed, you'll have my Black Stallion.[122]

He also discussed his admiration for Trevor (to whom he referred by her birth name, Chaille):

I feel that in Chaille you have the future of Brusally…Here you are with a great track record of your own in life, a great ranch and horses—and a short distance away you have working for you, loving you and Brusally, you have Chaille—so dedicated, so competent, beautiful on and off a horse… she and her beautifully trained horses are Brusally and the continuation, projection, of Ed Tweed's Brusally.[123]

Around that time, Farley visited Brusally Ranch and brought along his octogenarian friend Captain William "Bill" Heyer to watch Trevor ride. Heyer, a highly trained dressage and circus rider, had been head trainer for Ringling Bros. and Barnum & Bailey Circus. Farley noted that Heyer was "known throughout Europe as one of the truly great horsemen of the world" who "had performed in all the great circuses of Europe" and "was decorated by the kings of Sweden and Belgium; he also has a medal from Russia."[124] When Heyer saw Trevor ride Orzel, he commented to Farley that she was the best "lady rider he had seen in America" and that "she could become a high school, classic rider…Most important to Bill is 'feeling' and Chaille has it, along with her natural seat."[125]

Years later, Trevor wrote:

A rider learns to know his or her horse in a special way. Many qualities imperceptible to an observer become very real and important to a rider. Orzel feels unlike any other horse I have ridden. His tremendous power is coupled with balance and sensitivity. A rider has only to communicate clearly. He listens, responds, learns with amazing ease. He does not become angry or resentful. Above all, Orzel has heart: that bottomless reserve of inspired energy that thrills rider and spectator alike. In Polish, Orzel means "eagle," and the eagle is strong in him. He is proud, precise, secure in his supremacy—a study of immense power and perfectly synchronized motion.

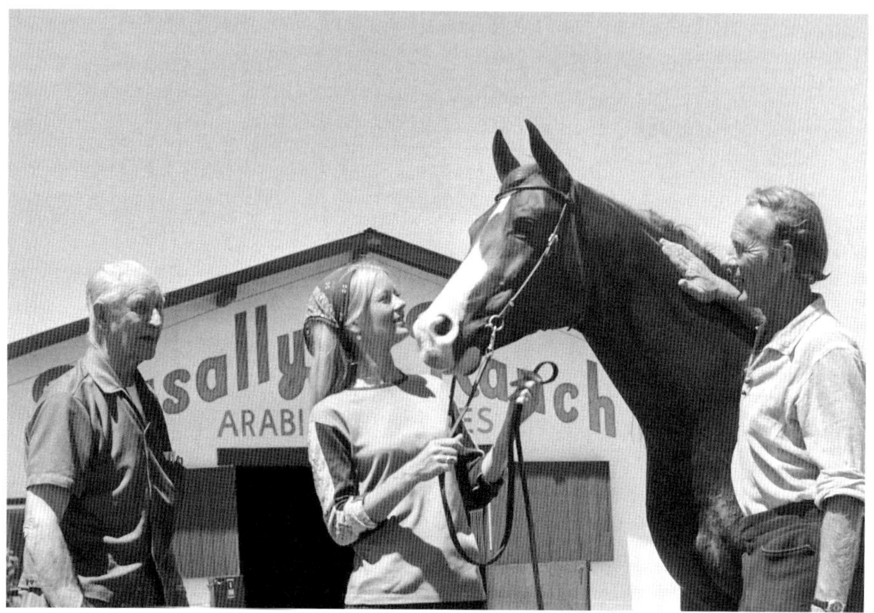

Trevor presents Orzel to dressage trainer Captain William "Bill" Heyer and Walter Farley, author of *The Black Stallion. Courtesy of Shelley Groom Trevor.*

Our favorite place to work is the track, where he soars on a natural high and never fails to draw me into his spell.[126]

At the February 1973 Scottsdale Show, Orzel was awarded the coveted Legion of Merit, which recognized his stellar achievements as a show horse. Three months later, at the Oklahoma All Arabian Horse Show, judged by Thomas C. Townsend, Orzel won the English pleasure championship over eight rivals, including his daughter Brusally Orzelyna.

Orzel's next English pleasure championship win took place in June at the North Texas All-Arabian Horse Show in Dallas, judged by Mrs. Howard Funderburgh and Bill Harris. Orzel triumphed over twenty-one other competitors, while Brusally Orzelyna won the English pleasure mares class, also over twenty-one rivals.

The next month, Orzel and his yearling son Brusally Orstar competed at the combined Sierra Empire All-Arabian Show and Region 1 Championship Show in Pomona, California, judged by Joseph Beyer and Tom McNair. Orzel was the English pleasure reserve champion of the Sierra Empire Show and named Region 1 Top Five English Pleasure. Brusally Orstar won the yearling colt class, with twenty-four entries,

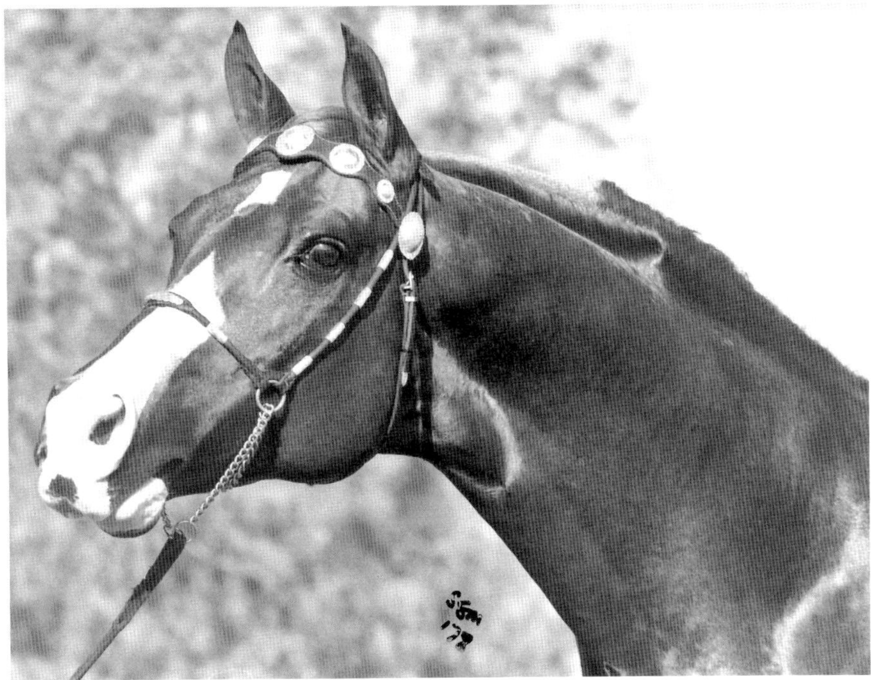

Orzel's eyes revealed what Trevor called his "mysterious wise mind." *Photo by S. Gail Miller, courtesy of Shelley Groom Trevor.*

and was named the junior reserve champion stallion of the Sierra Empire Show.

August found Orzel back in Oklahoma City again, competing in English pleasure at the 1973 U.S. National Championships, judged by Don Burt, Peter Cameron and Thomas C. Townsend. Raffon was named National Champion in English pleasure, with Basquelle the Reserve National Champion. Ridden by Trevor, Orzel finished among the Top Ten, along with Luminesque, Hy An Gay, Ramaseyn, Ramaraaas of Delta C, Rif Et Ref, Luzja and Fad Sue Zan. Brusally Orzelyna, also ridden by Trevor, became the first of Orzel's offspring to garner a national title when she was named U.S. National Top Ten English Pleasure.

From the time she was introduced to riding sidesaddle by Braswell, Trevor found herself drawn to this most feminine type of riding in which women, dressed in gowns, ride elegant, responsive mounts. However, for a number of years, a sidesaddle class was held only at the larger shows in which Trevor competed. Happily for her, in 1974, the first ladies' sidesaddle class was to be offered that summer at the U.S. National Championships in Albuquerque,

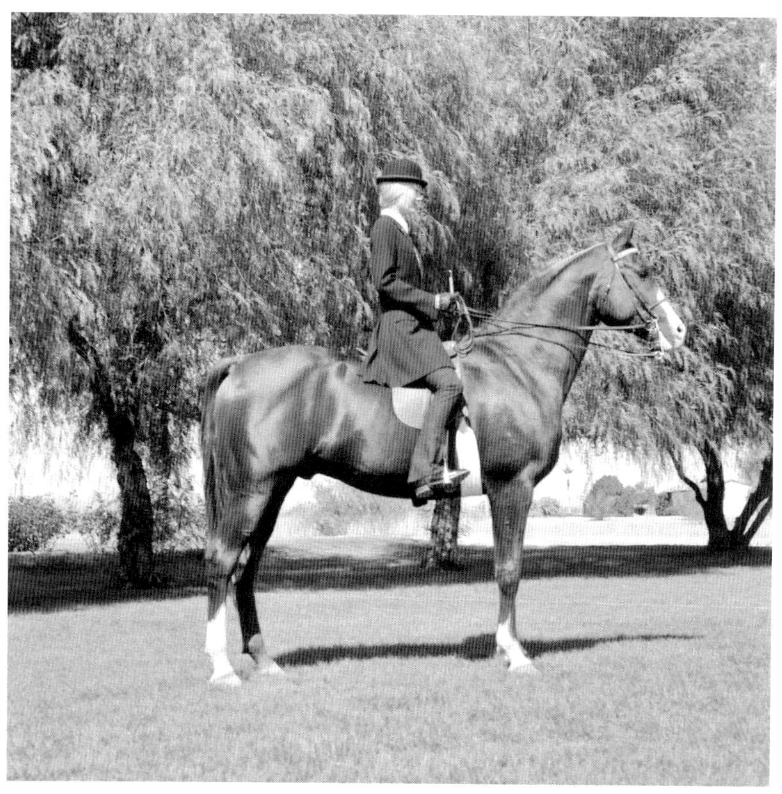

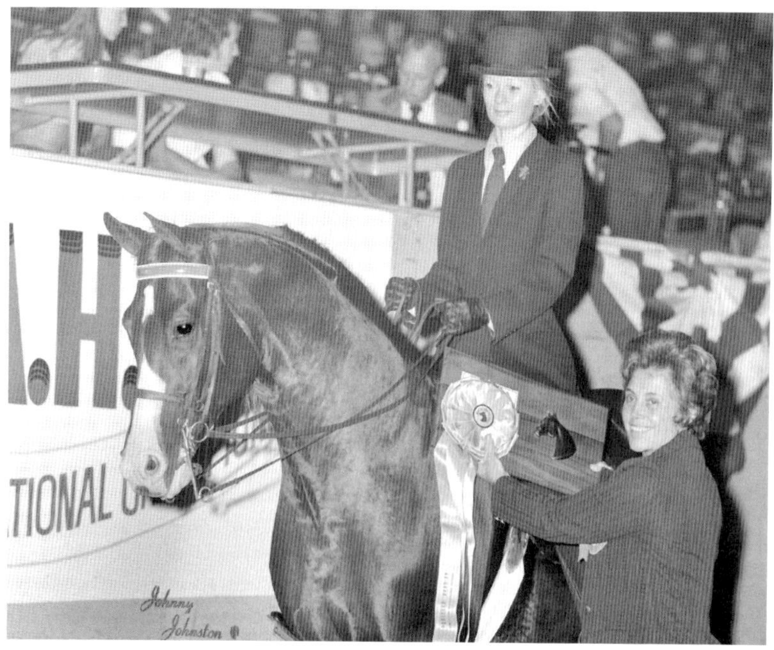

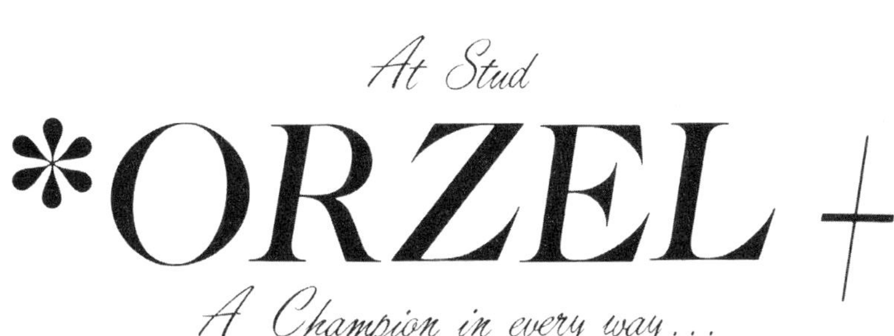

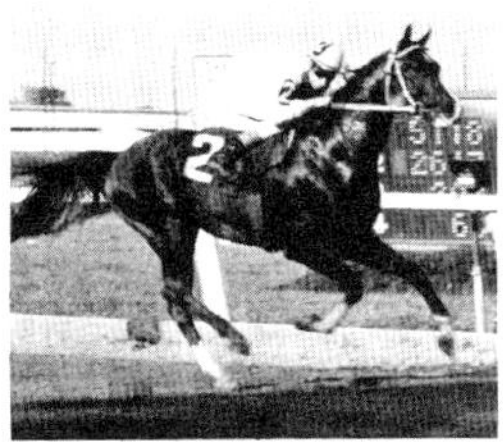

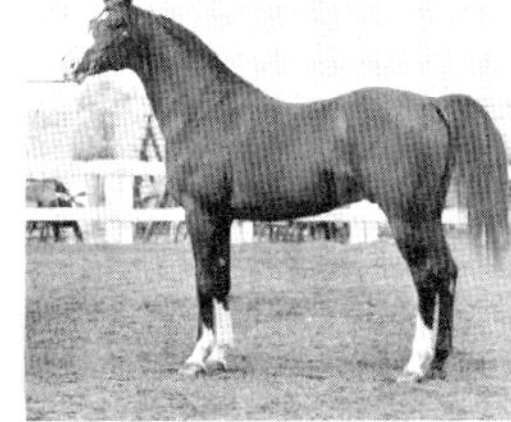

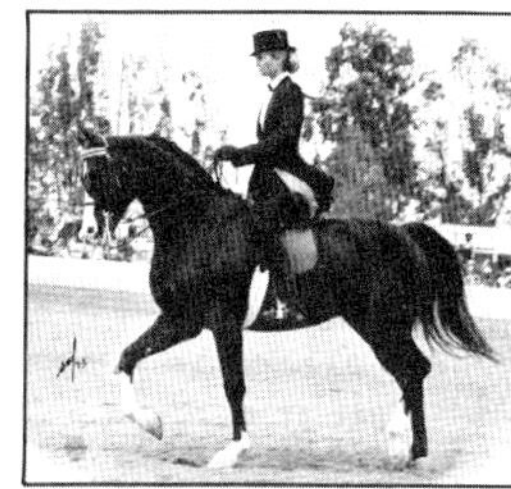

A 1973 advertisement for Orzel. *Courtesy of Shelley Groom Trevor.*

Opposite, top: Shelley Groom Trevor on Orzel. *Courtesy of Shelley Groom Trevor.*

Opposite, bottom: Orzel and Trevor are named 1973 U.S. National Top Ten in English pleasure. *Photo by Johnny Johnston, courtesy of Shelley Groom Trevor*

New Mexico. In February 1974, Trevor and Orzel won the ladies' sidesaddle class at the Scottsdale Show, and in August, Orzel became the recipient of the first U.S. National Champion Ladies' Sidesaddle title. Over the decades, Trevor's national championship ride on Orzel has become legendary. Arabian breeder Joe Cassel remembered that "this big, magnificent stallion floated into the ring with a petite, perfect rider melding together as one to form the most beautiful picture imaginable. Whether he was walking,

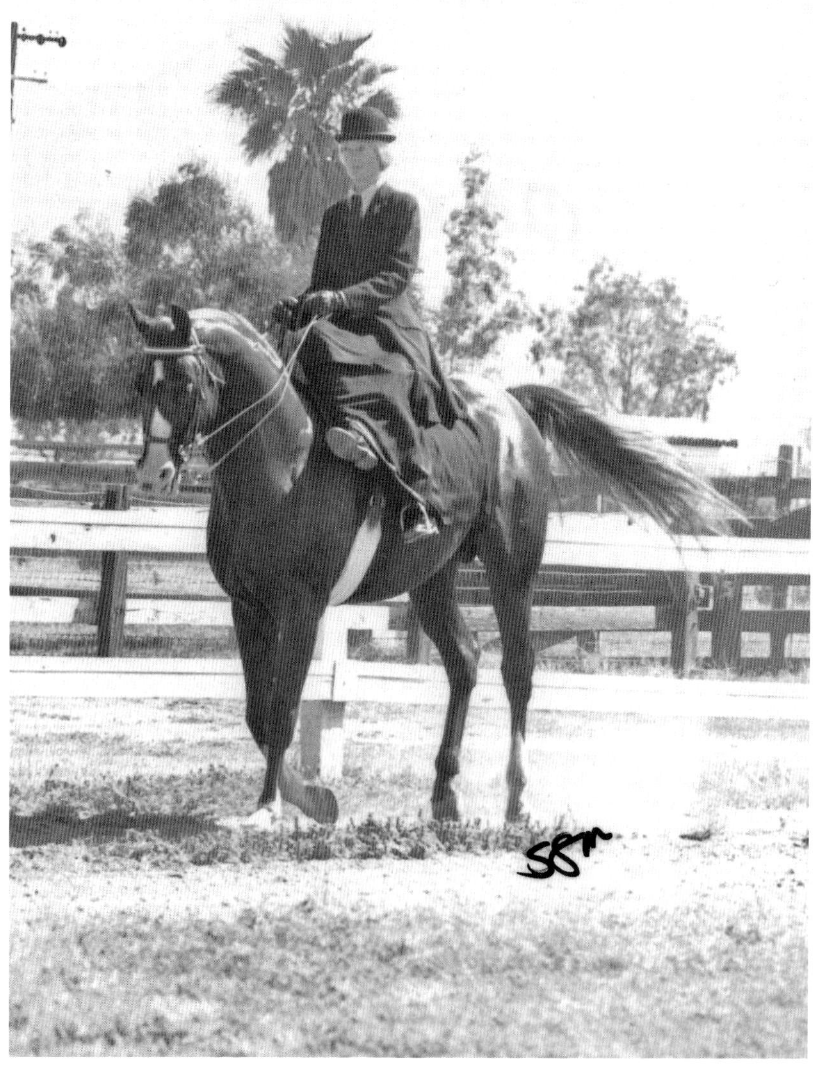

Trevor riding Orzel sidesaddle. *Photo by S. Gail Miller, courtesy of Shelley Groom Trevor.*

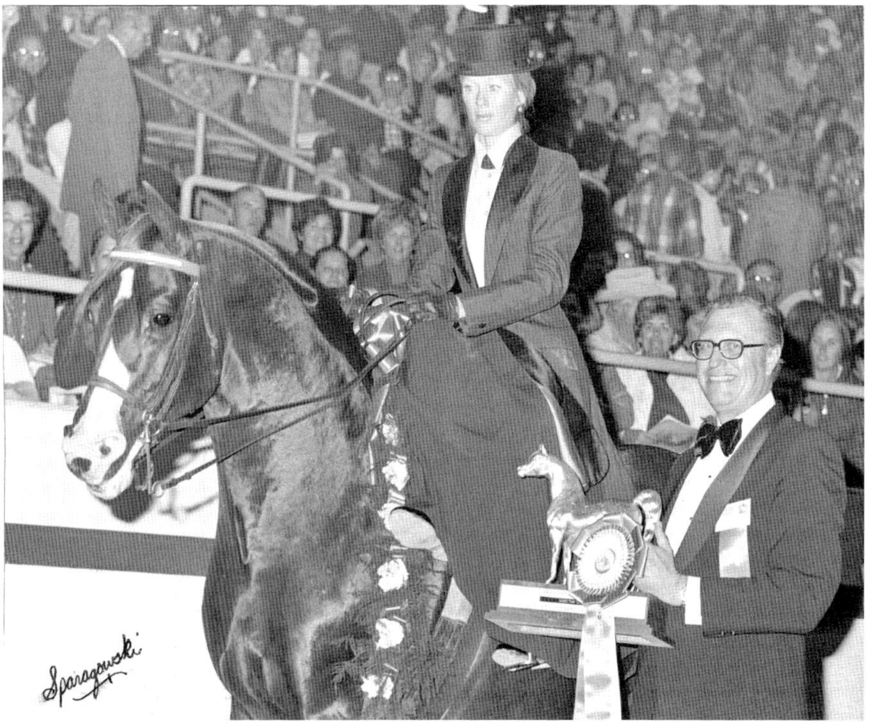

Orzel and Trevor are named 1974 U.S. National Champion Ladies' Sidesaddle. *Photo by Jerry Sparagowski, courtesy of Shelley Groom Trevor.*

trotting, or cantering, it was the same floating glide around the ring. A quiet hush was in the air as the crowd [sensed] this was a sight that perhaps would never be repeated."[127] And Gary Clay, a respected Scottsdale breeder, rider, trainer and horse show judge, remarked decades later that this ride was still "one of the finest performances I have ever seen."[128]

Orzel's last big win was at the 1976 International Arabian Horse Fair in Reno, Nevada, where he was named, once again, ladies' sidesaddle champion. The stallion was now thirteen years old. From 1966 to 1968, Orzel had won races in two countries, at distances ranging from just under a mile to more than one and a half miles. He had run successfully on both dirt tracks and turf courses and had defeated talented older horses, including multiple-stakes winners Kontiki, Pien and Wosk. He had been conditioned by three trainers, had been ridden by a series of different jockeys and had carried steadily increasing weight, up to 142 pounds—more than Man O' War or Secretariat ever did. In the show ring, he had garnered numerous championships, had been named a National Top Ten Stallion in the United States and Canada, had won National Top Ten honors in English pleasure and had been crowned a National Champion in two very distinct disciplines: racing and sidesaddle. There was nothing else for him to prove as a racehorse, a halter horse or a performance horse. It was time for his sons and daughters to make their mark in the Arabian world.

Chapter 6

A SUCCESSION OF STARS

A few weeks after his triumph over Kontiki at Turf Paradise, Orzel embarked on his stud career. To get him off to a good start, Tweed chose two of his best Polish mares to breed to him: Oaks winner Abhazja, as well as Gontyna, a race winner that had finished in the money in fourteen of her sixteen starts. Orzel also had piqued the interest of breeder Ruth R. Simms, wife of former New Mexico governor John F. Simms, who arranged for her mare El Wicu Naja, which had been a top cutting horse, to be bred to Tweed's racing star.

Orzel's first crop, which arrived in 1969, consisted of three foals, all of which would go on to successful careers. Simms's mare produced EW Gwee-zel, a Western pleasure champion that was also named Regional Top Five Stock. Abhazja foaled Brusally Oraba, which became a successful broodmare and was the granddam of a race winner and three national winners, including the impressive stallion Annapolis (which, as of this writing, has garnered an astounding eight National Champion titles, eight Reserve National Champion awards and eighteen National Top Tens). However, the star of the crop was decidedly Gontyna's filly, Brusally Orzelyna. Trained and ridden by Shelley Groom Trevor, the 15.1-hand mare became Orzel's first national winner, with two U.S. National Top Ten titles in Western pleasure. Orzelyna was also a champion in halter and English pleasure. In the mid-1970s, when Trevor became interested in dressage, she trained Orzelyna in the discipline and showed her in third- and fourth-level dressage classes, sometimes competing against her talented younger brother Brusally

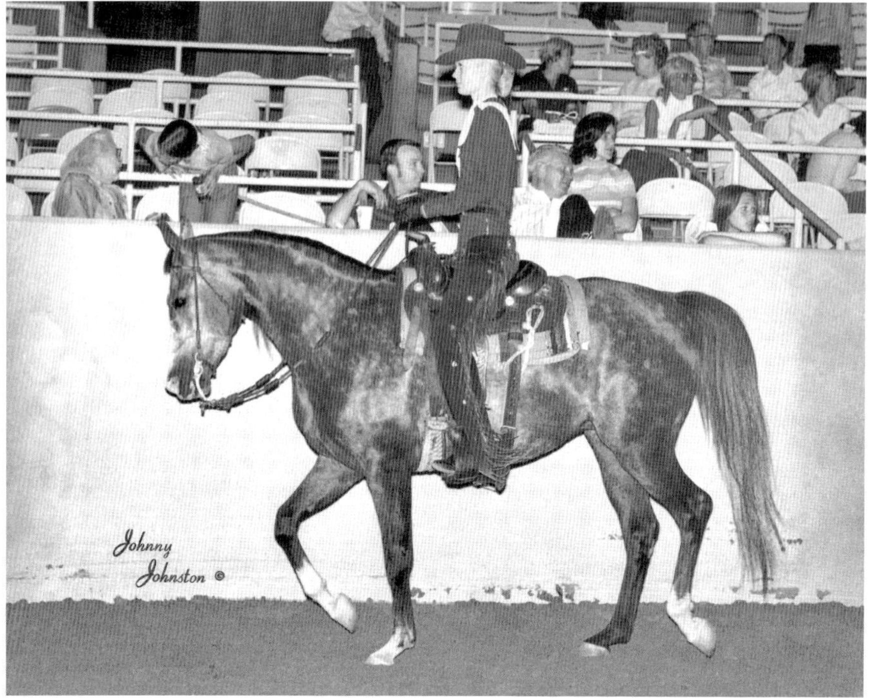

Ridden by Trevor, Brusally Orzelyna was named U.S. National Top Ten in Western pleasure in 1973 and 1975. *Photo by Johnny Johnston, courtesy of Shelley Groom Trevor.*

Orzetyn. Calling her "an elegant and feminine version of Orzel," Trevor noted that Orzelyna, like her brother, was a remarkably easy horse to train.[129]

Four foals were born in 1970. Not surprisingly, Gontyna was bred again to Orzel, producing Western pleasure winner and sire Brusally-Orzelyn, purchased from Tweed by former Missouri state senator Marvin Singleton. Orzelyn sired only six foals before his early death at age nine; he was the grandsire of one national winner. Tweed's imported race winner Bulawa produced the lovely mare Brusally Orzelawa, a Western pleasure champion that measured 15.2 hands. Orzelawa was the dam of two national winners. Miroluba and Chlosta, two daughters of the racing sire Faher, produced foals by Orzel that would greatly influence Arabian racing even though they themselves did not race. Miroluba's daughter Brusally Orzeluba was the dam of Bask-O-Zel, a U.S. National Champion Racehorse; Magna Terra Macho, a Racehorse of the Year; one stakes winner; and two race winners. Chlosta's son Brusally Orzelost, a 15.2½-hand stallion, sired twenty-eight race winners and five stakes winners, among them KA Czubuthan, an influential breeding stallion nicknamed "the big red stud" for his great resemblance to his grandsire.

Orzel's 1971 crop consisted of six foals, three of them from the Brusally mares Gontyna, Miroluba and Wislica and three from mares owned by others. Of these six foals, two were national winners, two produced national winners, four produced race winners and two produced stakes winners. Brusally Orzetyn, the third foal from the Orzel-Gontyna cross, was a flashy chestnut colt that caught Trevor's eye at a young age. She saw him "moving in his paddock with that certain grace that sets one individual apart from another." When the time came to train him, "it was as though he already knew, and already had, all the necessary talents. I had only to give aids clearly, and step by step he progressed into an extremely sensitive, agile, and honest horse."[130] Trevor first pointed Orzetyn toward a career in English pleasure, but she found herself growing disenchanted with the way Arabians were being shown in English pleasure and other "action" classes. "A tense, artificial way of going wasn't my style," she declared. Around that time, the Hungarian dressage master Charles de Kunffy began traveling to Scottsdale to give periodic clinics to a small group of local dressage riders, and Trevor decided to attend, riding Orzetyn. De Kunffy "tried at first, somewhat unsuccessfully, to put my saddleseat position into dressage form," she noted, "while Orzetyn proceeded brilliantly." Trevor became a convert to dressage, which, she said, "gave me insight into the subtle biomechanical communication between horse and rider." Trevor later trained with Andrew Popiel, an eventing rider from Canada:

> *Under Andrew's guidance, Orzetyn and I progress*[ed] *not only as dressage competitors but as jumpers too. Orzetyn has always been one of those horses who never finds any cause to be nervous and who never stops thinking. From the beginning, what he lacked in experience he made up for in agility and in the ability to think his way over a fence.…No other horse has given me such feelings of joy and freedom in undertaking anything.*[131]

In 1980, Brusally Orzetyn was named U.S. National Champion Third Level Dressage. He was ultimately shown at the Prix St. Georges level in dressage, competed at the novice level in eventing and also showed in Western riding, English pleasure, jumping, native costume and sidesaddle classes.

The other national winner in the 1971 crop was Mohawk Chief, owned by Robert S. Gay, a Michigan breeder who had done well in the show ring with a number of Brusally-related horses. A tall, athletic chestnut

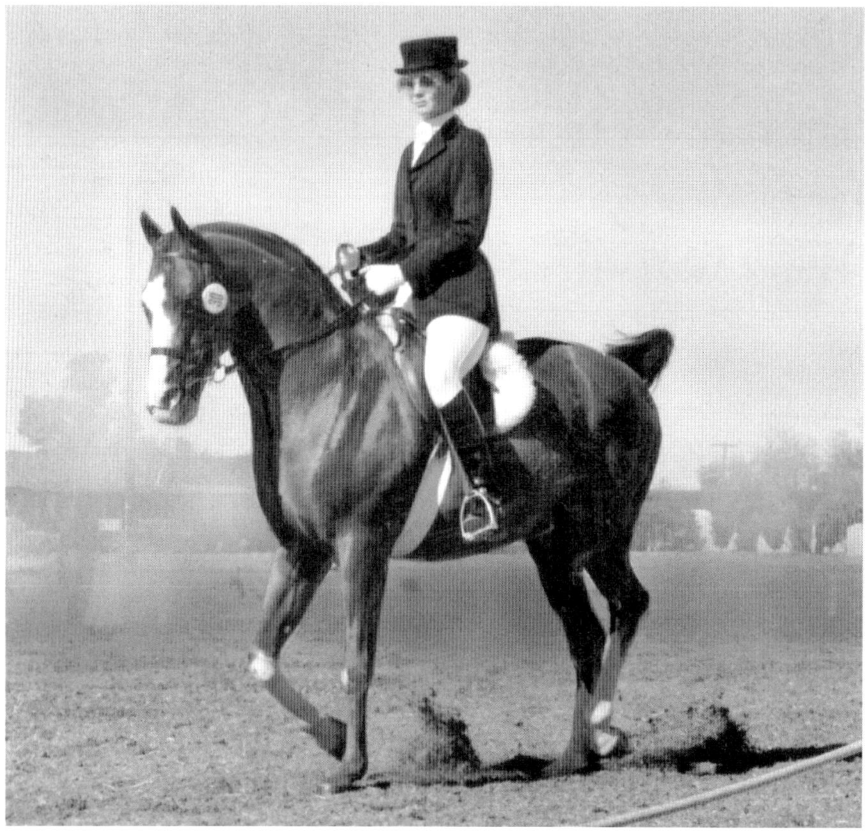

Ridden by Trevor, Brusally Orzetyn was 1980 U.S. National Champion Third Level Dressage. *Courtesy of Shelley Groom Trevor.*

stallion with markings reminiscent of his father's, Mohawk Chief excelled in sidesaddle competition. With Trevor aboard, he was named 1978 U.S. National Top Ten Ladies' Sidesaddle. As a breeding stallion, Mohawk Chief sired Indian Jewel, a mare that garnered three national titles in the hunter division, and was the grandsire of Asadya, Canadian National Champion Informal Combination.

Eight foals by Orzel were born in 1972, and as with the previous crop, two of these offspring became national winners. The colt Brusally Orzelaw was a race winner that ran for three seasons; the gelding Brusally Orlin became a winning event horse; and another gelding, Brusally Orzelon, was trained in dressage by well-known rider Major Edward Renom, of the Argentine cavalry. The promising Brusally Orstar, which was named the junior reserve champion stallion of the Sierra Empire Show in 1973, died the following year. Brusally

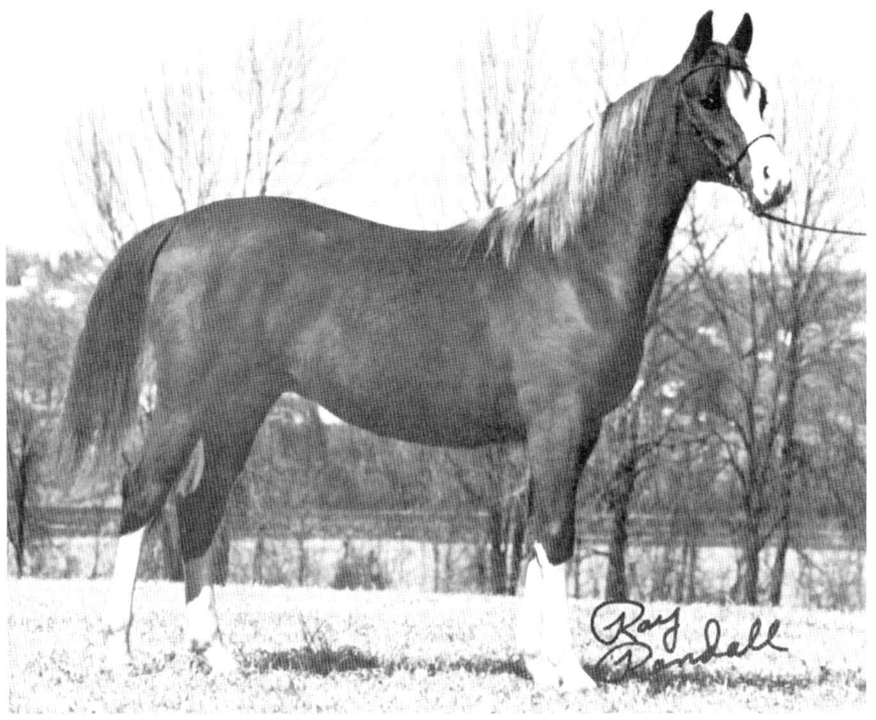

Mohawk Chief, ridden by Trevor, was 1978 U.S. National Top Ten Ladies' Sidesaddle. *Photo by Ray Randall, courtesy of Shelley Groom Trevor.*

Orenka and Brusally Orzelsta became excellent broodmares; the latter was the dam of seven race winners and one stakes winner. Arazel, bred and owned by J. Kipp and Susan Charlton of Bar Keema Ranch in Arizona, was named 1975 U.S. National Champion Futurity Gelding and later garnered three U.S. National Top Ten Gelding awards. He also was Scottsdale champion gelding on three occasions. With the Charltons' daughter Cindy, Arazel won many English pleasure championships. He was awarded the Legion of Supreme Merit and became a member of *Arabian Horse World* magazine's Four-Star Gelding Club. In a 1979 article, his owners remarked:

> *Besides being a bold and powerful horse in the ring, Arazel fulfills the need for companionship. An alert and cheerful face greets us each day at the barn. Often he joins our other horses at Bar Keema and sets out for the fun trail rides, leaving the pressure of the show ring for the beauty and quiet of the desert. This is an important time for all of us, where the thrill and enjoyment of owning a horse such as "Ari" are truly realized.*[132]

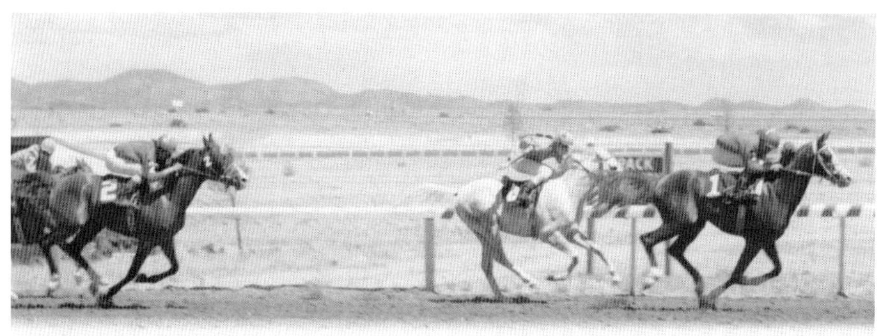

Brusally Orzelaw winning at Santa Fe Downs in 1976. *Courtesy of Shelley Groom Trevor.*

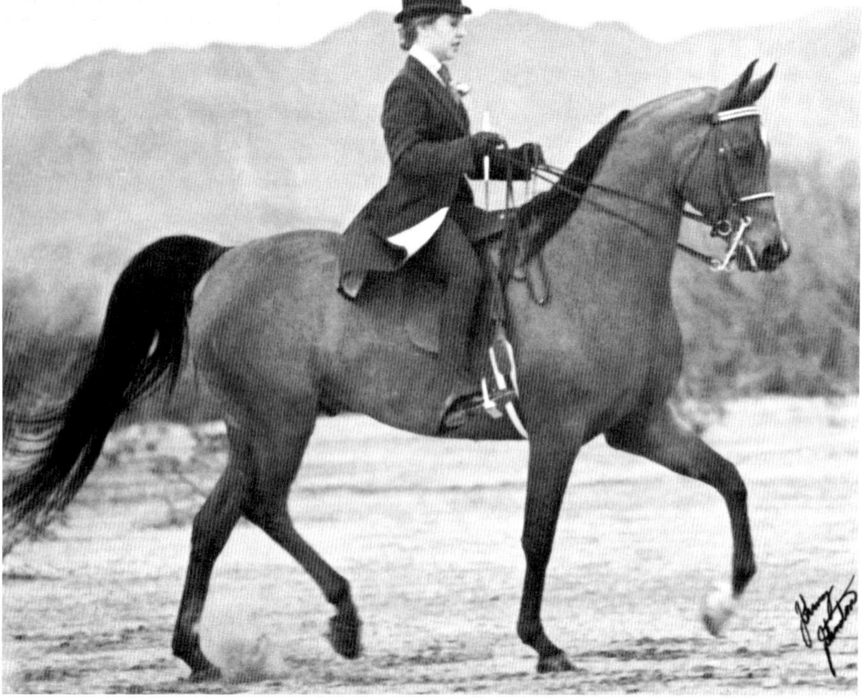

Arazel, ridden here by Cindy Charlton, won four national titles, including 1975 U.S. National Champion Futurity Gelding. *Photo by Johnny Johnston, courtesy of Shelley Groom Trevor.*

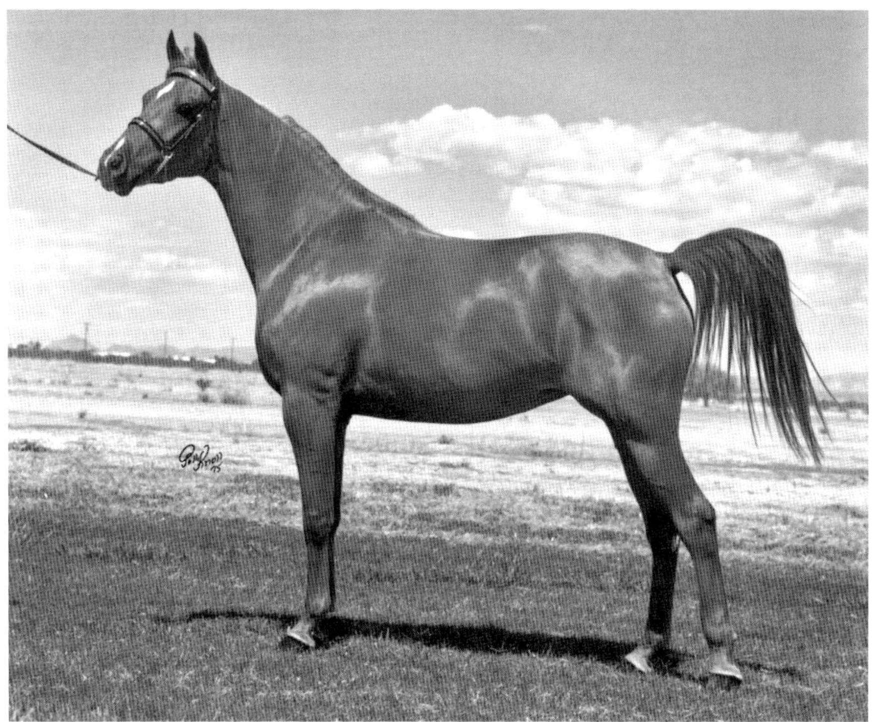

Brusally Orzelta was 1978 Canadian National Reserve Champion Stock and 1978 and 1980 U.S. National Top Ten Stock. *Photo by Polly Knoll, courtesy of Shelley Groom Trevor.*

Brusally Orzelta, the second national winner in the 1972 crop, was a chestnut filly out of Skoretta, a daughter of Tweed's favorite, Skorage. "Bo," as she was called, was named 1978 Canadian Reserve National Champion Stock and was also twice U.S. National Top Ten Stock. Her trainer/rider, Gary Clay, remembered Orzelta as a "cool mare" that was "very talented," and a 1978 advertisement prior to the mare's Canadian Nationals win noted that "Orzelta is a big, chestnut mare who is ideally built for her role as a top Western horse."[133]

The 1973 crop was Orzel's largest one yet, with eleven foals. Standouts included a national winner, a Race Colt of the Year, a regional reserve champion and the producers of three race winners and one stakes winner: CR Samborsta, Darley Champion Three-Year-Old Filly. Brusally Orin, the last foal of Tweed's lovely imported broodmare Algorina, was a tall and athletic gray gelding with an excellent saddle position and long shoulder. Between 1981 and 1986, this gifted jumper won a total of seven National Top Ten awards in the hunter division and was awarded the Legion of

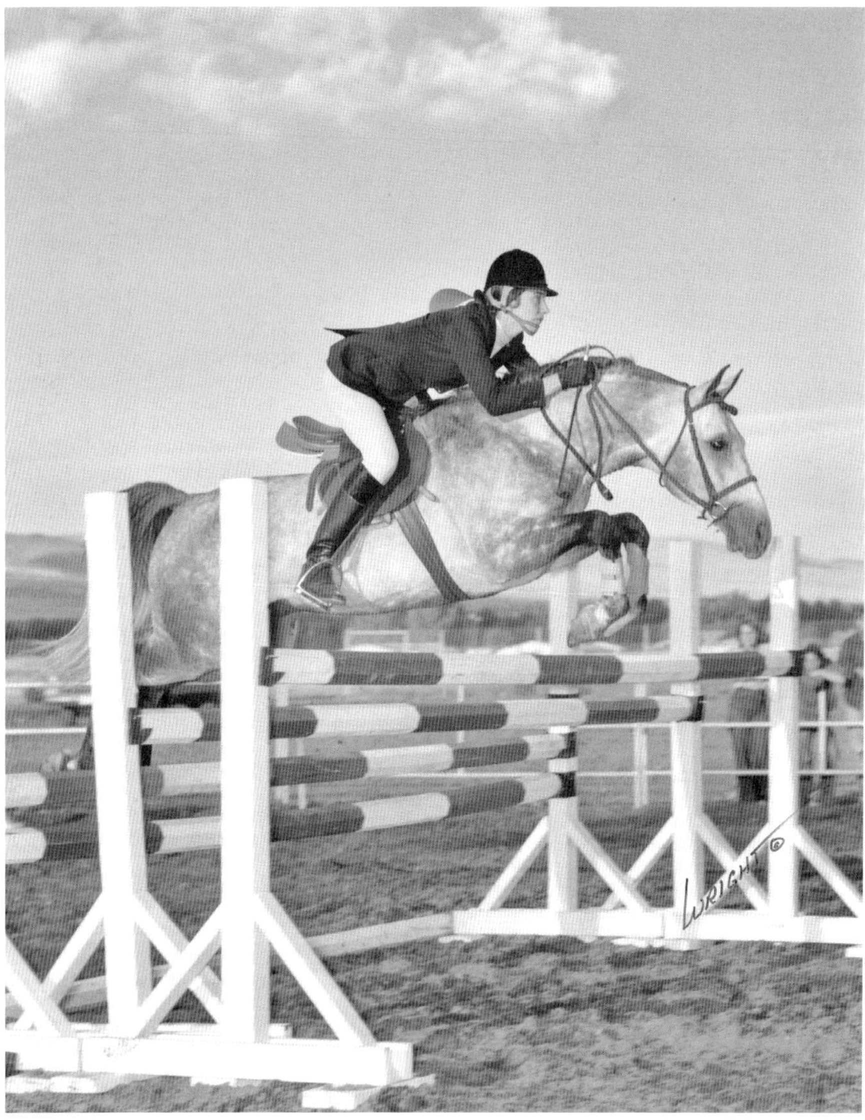

Brusally Orin, ridden here by Joyce Kegley, won seven U.S. or Canadian National Top Ten awards in the hunter division. *Photo by Wright, courtesy of Shelley Groom Trevor.*

Honor. Interestingly, two of Orin's Top Ten placings were in hunter over fences classes, in which his "niece," Indian Jewel (by the Orzel son Mohawk Chief), was also named to the Top Ten.

The other noteworthy individual among the 1973 foals was Ormir, yet another good example of the Orzel-Miroluba cross. This big bay colt, which ran four times, winning twice and finishing second once, was named 1976 Race Colt of the Year. Unfortunately, Ormir died at age four, having sired only seven purebred foals.

The year 1974 saw the arrival of five foals by Orzel. Of these, the only notable individual was Jarzel, a Western pleasure amateur to ride champion. This crop was unusual in that, for the first time, none of the mares bred to Orzel was a Polish import. There were a couple of reasons for this. First, Orzel was now competing with his stablemate Zbrucz and the young stallion Brusally Farbast for breedings to Tweed's imported Polish mares. And second, some of the Brusally mares, both Polish and domestic, that had nicked well with Orzel in the past had been sold or had died. These included Algorina, Nawojka, Skoretta and Star of Erka. It was also becoming clear that Orzel's best foals from his first crops came almost exclusively from a small group of mares, mostly of Polish racing lines. "Orzel was tricky to breed," conceded Trevor, whereas "Zbrucz was our most consistent sire. You could walk into a pasture and pick out the Zbrucz babies." Compared to Orzel's offspring, the Zbrucz foals were faster to mature, more reactive and more refined, and they often inherited their sire's extravagant park trot—making them easier to sell at a young age, particularly to those show-oriented Arabian fanciers who prized high-energy movement above all. However, the horsemen and women who were willing to wait for the Orzel foals to mature almost always discovered that they possessed substance, riding-horse conformation, athletic ability, a stable temperament and three excellent gaits. Trevor also noted that although Orzel did not cross well with a wide spectrum of mares, his foals from particular broodmares—such as Chlosta, Gontyna and Miroluba—were consistently superb.[134] What was not known, at this point, was how successful Orzel would later be, when bred to daughters of Zbrucz, which contributed their sire's elegance and freer movement to the attributes that Orzel himself passed on. In the meantime, while waiting for Zbrucz's daughters to mature, Tweed would continue to experiment with mares of different bloodlines to see which ones worked well with Orzel.

The 1975 crop consisted of four foals. Three of them were produced by mares of predominantly domestic breeding, while one was out of a daughter of the Polish import Faraon. Between them, the three daughters of Orzel went on to produce one regional winner, two champions and six race winners. Five of these six race winners were produced by Farazel, out of Brusally Faronifa, by Faraon. Interestingly, the mare Summer, out of a daughter of National Champion Ibn Fadjur, was exported to Brazil, where she produced five foals. Twenty-five years after Summer was foaled, a granddaughter of hers,

NNL Scandal Nashana, was imported from Brazil to the United States, where she was later named U.S. National Top Ten Arabian Mare Breeding Adult Amateur to Handle and went on to create her own dynasty of national winners.

Ten foals were born in 1976, including Tamor-Zel, which garnered five regional titles in Western pleasure and reining and was awarded the Legion of Supreme Honor; Kona Queen, champion Western pleasure junior horse; Royal Orzel, an English pleasure champion; a filly out of Chlosta, Brusaly [*sic*] Orzelosta, which later produced two race winners; Brusally Orselar, out of the Polish race winner Cerera, which went on to sire four race winners; and Cassels Orzel, out of a granddaughter of Algorina, which also sired four race winners. The best-known member of this crop, however, is Magus, whose dam was of primarily English breeding. Initially used as trail horse, the chestnut stallion eventually came into the hands of the racehorse owners and breeders Scott and Carolyn Gipson, who began using Magus on race-bred mares when he was fourteen. "When the foals arrived the next year," wrote Carolyn, "we were very pleased, very pleased with what we saw, and bred him to three more of our mares. We all know that when breeding for the racetrack, the foals can be great looking, but you don't really know if they have talent until they actually run. It was a long four years from breeding to racing, but we learned a lot from that year's foal crop…Magus was a racehorse sire."[135] In total, Magus sired four stakes winners and eleven race winners and was the grandsire of five stakes winners and seventeen race winners.

The year 1977 saw the arrival of eight foals, including DW Orzefar, a champion reining horse; race winner Otiki, out of a daughter of Orzel's great rival, Kontiki; and the English pleasure winner Orzan, Orzel's first foal out of a Zbrucz daughter. Bred again to one of his old standbys, Miroluba, Orzel sired Babe, which went on to produce five race winners. And bred to his own daughter, Brusally Orzelyna, Orzel sired Brusally Orlyna, the dam of three race winners—one by Zbrucz, one by a son of Zbrucz and one by a grandson of Kontiki.[136]

The 1978 crop consisted of five foals. Among them was Brusally Orzelast, a race winner whose dam was a daughter of Zbrucz and Chlosta. Orzelast was also the sire of one race winner and one stakes winner. The flashy gelding Cerazel, out of Cerera, was a fixture at shows in Scottsdale during the 1980s. He was a reserve champion in Western pleasure amateur owner to ride and had wins in English pleasure amateur owner to ride, pleasure driving and trail classes. And BR Gay Contessa, out of a daughter of Zbrucz and Tweed's Polish mare Salinaa, produced Detroit, Canadian National Champion Futurity Colt, and Sandcastle, Regional Champion

Hunter Pleasure Amateur to Ride. Gay Contessa was also the granddam of one race winner, one stakes winner and national winners in second-level dressage, native costume and hunter pleasure.

In 1979, Orzel sired three foals, all out of Zbrucz daughters. Notably, Brusally Oryna was the dam of two race winners and granddam of a

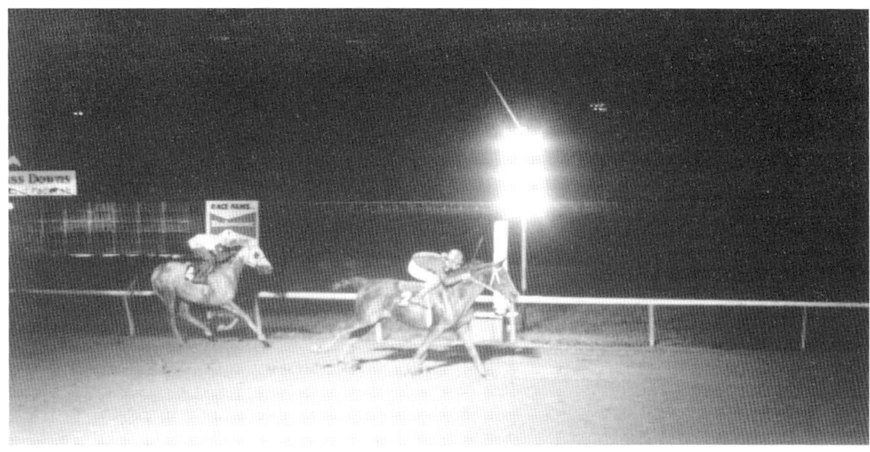

Oct 1,1988
6 Fur/ 1:25.1
Place: Kuegar Kon
Show: Zeitawi Shadatyr

Brusally Orlen
Owner: Brian Braithwaite
Trainer: Owner
Up: Kim Fredericks

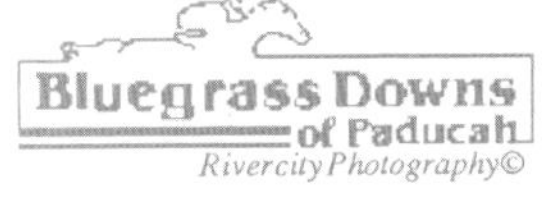

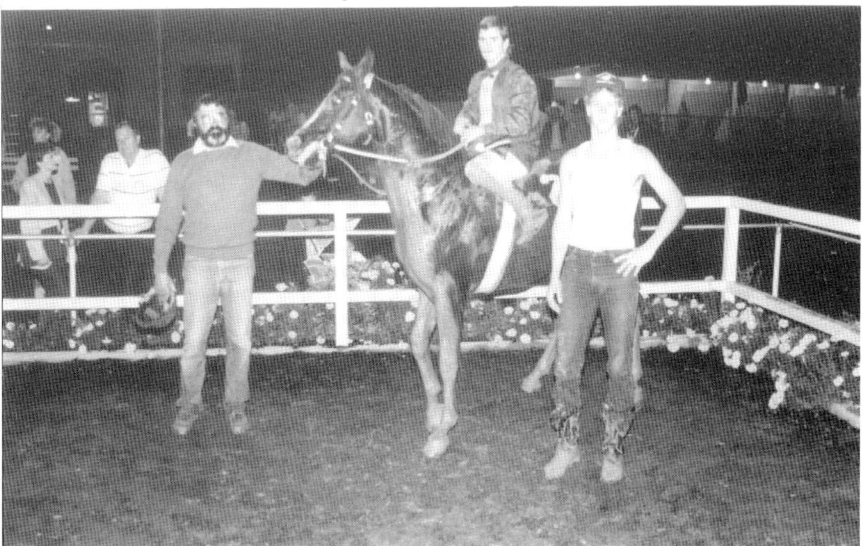

Brusally Orlen winning at Bluegrass Downs in 1988. *Courtesy of Shelley Groom Trevor.*

regional winner in English pleasure and a champion in Country English pleasure, while Orzels Zbrusalyna produced a Regional Top Five Hunter Pleasure winner.

Five foals were born in 1980, two of them produced by daughters of Zbrucz. The standout of this crop was Brusally Orlen, a stakes winner that ran for four years, winning six of nineteen starts and finishing in the money seventeen times. Trevor considered him one of Orzel's most athletic sons. Orlen was a sensational sire of racehorses and endurance horses, often when bred to mares with Orzel in their pedigrees by way of Brusally Orzetyn. Among his offspring are RD Zell, a Darley Champion Sprinter; Zachzell, a Darley Champion Older Horse; and stakes winner LZP Heluvazell, as well as five race winners. Orlen was the grandsire of four stakes winners and twenty-three race winners. Orlen's descendants are also known for their abilities as endurance horses; for instance, competitors such as Juanazel and LD Crystal Lite each logged more than two thousand miles, and Double Zell and Orzo are credited with more than three thousand miles apiece.

The 1981 crop of four foals was full of racing talent. Orzel's last foal out of Chlosta, race winner SMR Ibn Orzel, sired one stakes winner and sixteen race winners. Brusally Orzaborr, out of a daughter of Bulawa, was a Western pleasure reserve champion. He was the sire of one race winner and grandsire of three race winners, two stakes winners and a gelding named Noing, which garnered six national titles in trail classes and won the Legion of Honor. Race winner Brusally Zelyna, a three-quarter sister to national winners Brusally Orzetyn and Brusally Orzelyna, was a Race Mare of the Year, produced two race winners and also was shown in dressage by Trevor. And Orzela, out of the well-known racer Fagai, won four stakes races and was the granddam of two race winners and three stakes winners. Carolyn Gipson recalled seeing Orzela, trained by her father, Chuck Tolbert, win the 1985 Gladys Brown Edwards Stakes: "She and another mare led the other seven horses (all colts) around the one-mile track to a close finish, with Orzela winning by a head. She was a tall, angular, magnificent mare [that was] the same fiery red color as Orzel himself."[137]

All four of Orzel's 1982 foals were out of Zbrucz daughters. SGR Valentina, sister of stakes winner SGR Vayu, was the dam of two race winners and granddam of another. Brusally Gazella, sister of race winner Brusally Zelyna, produced two race winners and was the granddam of one stakes winner and three race winners. And Brusally Orsata, sister of stakes winner Brusally Gaysar, foaled one race winner and was the granddam of two race winners and two stakes winners.

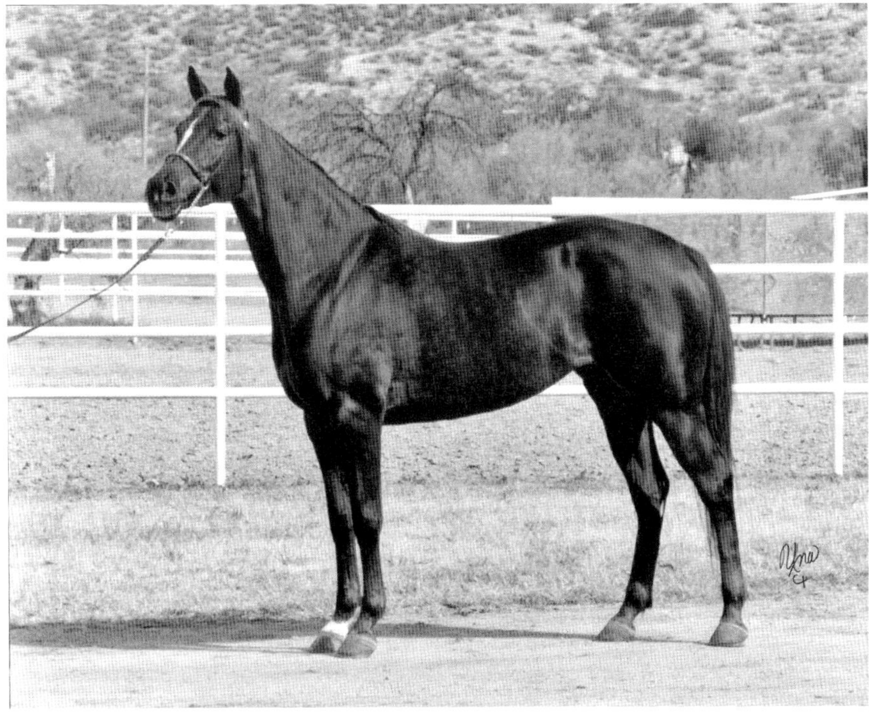

Brusally Zelyna was named 1986 U.S. Race Mare of the Year. *Courtesy of Shelley Groom Trevor.*

Eight foals were born in 1983, the year that Orzel turned twenty. This crop included two stakes winners, Brusally Gaysar and SGR Vayu, both out of Zbrucz mares. SGR Vayu later became a sire and grandsire of race winners; Vayu's son MVA Prince Vayu was exported to Poland, where he was used at stud by a private breeder and sired some race winners. Three outstanding broodmares were members of this crop: FMR Kasia (out of a Zbrucz daughter), the dam of one race winner and granddam of three more; Dakshina, sister of stakes winner Brusally Orlen, which produced one stakes winner and five race winners; and Gazella III (out of a daughter of Zbrucz), the dam of three race winners and granddam of seven race winners, including the Darley Award winner TM Super Bird and Sammy V, current holder of the record time for six furlongs in the United States.

In 1984, Orzel sired nine foals, including the stakes-winning gelding Worzel and race winners Ila (sister of Brusally Orlen), Orram and Orzel II. The latter became a useful sire of race winners and endurance horses, especially when bred to mares descended from Priboj. Two fillies out of Zbrucz mares, Brusally Ofirka and FMR Celebrate, produced numerous race and stakes

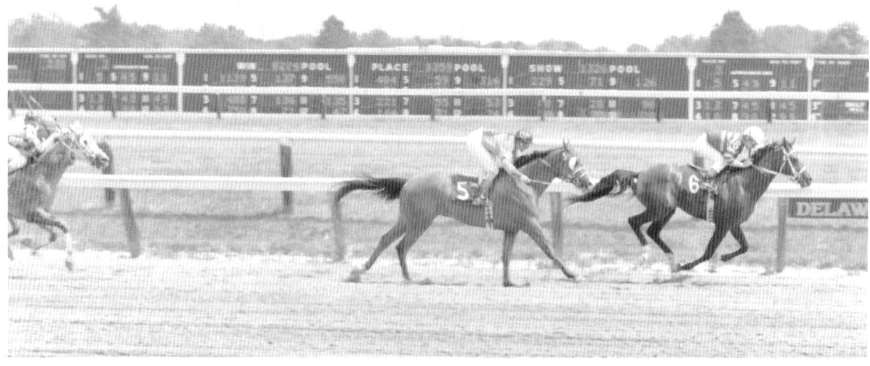

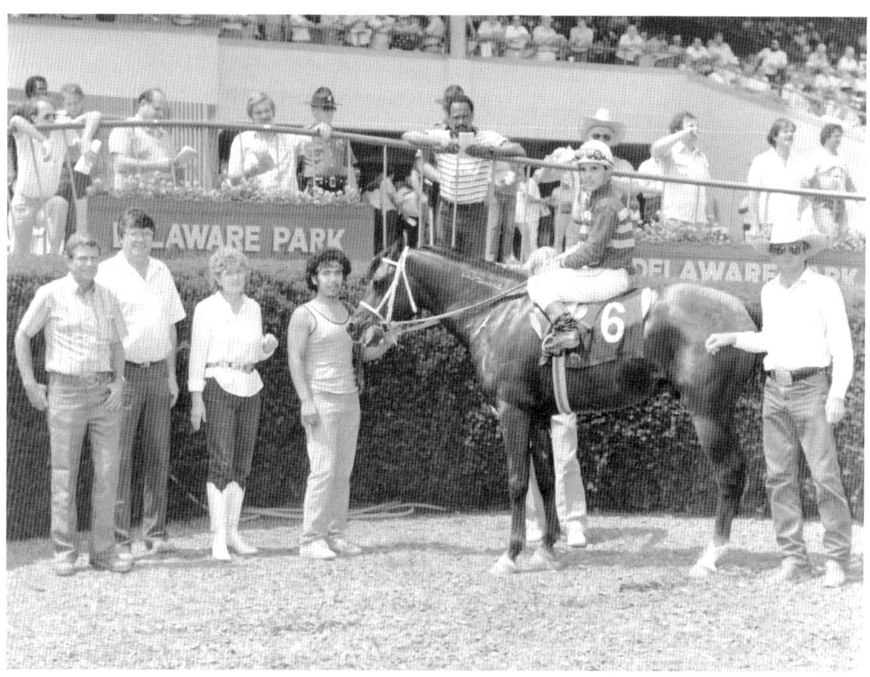

Brusally Gaysar winning at Delaware Park in 1986. *Courtesy of Shelley Groom Trevor.*

winners; FMR Celebrate was the dam of Horse of the Year FMR Hadassah. And, for the first time in both of their breeding careers, Orzel was bred to Genua, a Polish mare that was among Tweed's best producers; the resulting filly, FMR Grand Jubilee, became an excellent broodmare herself. Grand Jubilee foaled a race winner and a stakes winner and was the granddam

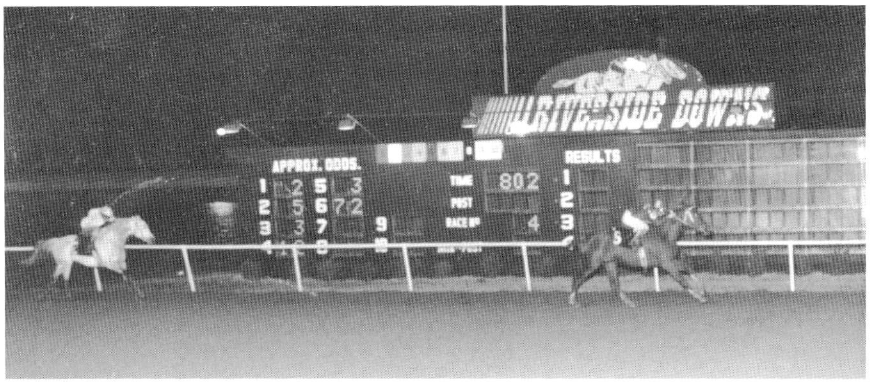

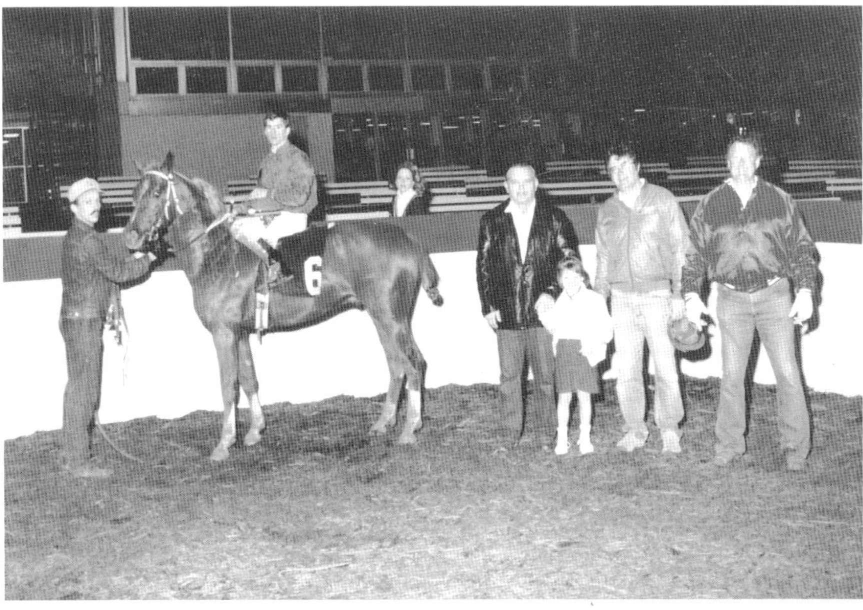

Orzel II winning at Riverside Downs in 1989. *Courtesy of Shelley Groom Trevor.*

of two stakes winners and four race winners, including the durable gelding Le Fromage, which started an incredible 113 times over a ten-year period, winning thirteen stakes races and amassing $190,317.

Orzel's 1985 crop—his last—consisted of one colt, the chestnut Orzelro, which was a non-winner on the track, competed as an endurance horse in

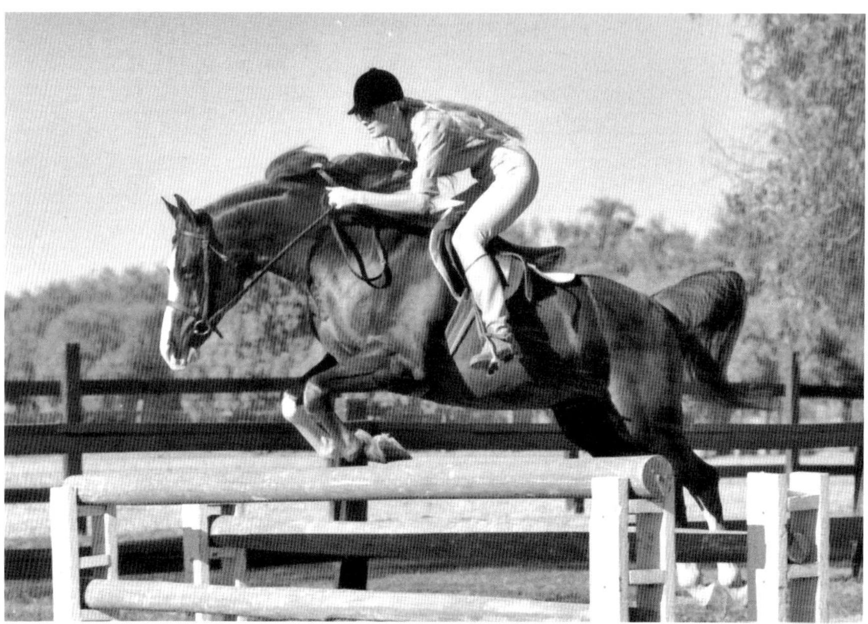

Brusally Orzetyn, ridden by Trevor, was one of two Orzel offspring that competed in eventing, which features three phases: dressage, show jumping and cross country. *Photo by Herb Wicks, courtesy of Shelley Groom Trevor.*

his teens and sired seven purebred foals, the last one when he was twenty-one years old.

In summary, from 1969 through 1985, Orzel sired seventeen crops of foals, for a total of ninety-eight purebred offspring and at least three part-bred foals.[138] Of these ninety-eight foals, nine were race winners and five were stakes winners. His daughter Brusally Zelyna was voted Race Mare of the Year, while his son Ormir was named Race Colt of the Year. In the show ring, two of his get were national champions (in halter and dressage), four were national winners (in Western pleasure, stock, hunter and sidesaddle), three were regional winners and five were show champions. Orzel was also the sire of two horses that participated in eventing and four that were trained in dressage, at a time when there were relatively few dressage shows and eventing horse trials being held in the United States. Two offspring are known to have competed in endurance riding.

Unlike some stallions, which make their marks through either their sons or their daughters, Orzel continues to influence Arabian breeding through both sides of the pedigree. Seventy-six of his ninety-eight purebred foals produced offspring. Orzel's most successful sons at stud include Brusally Orlen, Brusally

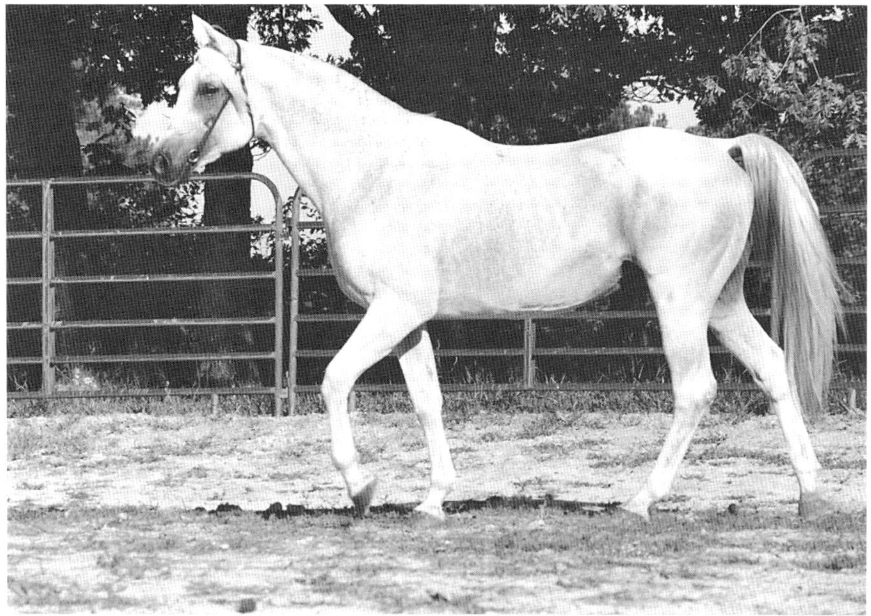

Brusally Orzelost was one of Orzel's best-siring sons. *Courtesy of Michael Economopoulos.*

Orzelost, Brusally Orzetyn, Magus, Orzel II and SMR Ibn Orzel. Five of his daughters were exported to other countries for use as broodmares: Babe to Canada; Brusally Gazella and Orzels Keepsake to Qatar; Orzela to France; and the aforementioned Summer to Brazil. Among Orzel's most influential daughters are Babe, BR Gay Contessa, Brusally Orzelawa, Brusally Orzeluba, Brusally Ormiro, Brusally Orsta, Dakshina, Farazel, FMR Celebrate, FMR Grand Jubilee and Gazella III.

Orzel was the grandsire of more than 1,000 foals, which include 136 race winners, 25 stakes winners, 5 national winners, 9 regional winners and 9 show champions. Of Orzel's grandget competing in endurance riding, 10 horses are credited with between 1,000 and 2,000 miles; three have logged between 2,000 and 3,000 miles; and one has racked up 3,475 miles.

In the last decade, Orzel's descendants have continued to excel in a variety of disciplines. To cite only a few highlights, in 2006, the Last Danse was the Darley Champion Three-Year-Old Colt. In 2007, MVA Scarlet Orzel was named U.S. National Champion Reining Horse, Junior to Ride. In 2008, the brothers Armanni and Annapolis were both named U.S. National Top Ten Sport Horse Stallions. The same year, the colt Abu Alemarat won the Dubai Triple Crown races, and the filly Zbroja Fata won Poland's Criterium Stakes.

In 2009, Mukata Fata won the Polish Oaks, and Double Zell completed the first of four consecutive Tevis Cup rides, up to 2012. In 2013, the twenty-two-year-old stallion Beymoon Zela was named U.S. National Champion Intermediare II Dressage and U.S. National Top Ten Grand Prix Dressage. In 2014, RB Champagne Taste was crowned the Darley Four-Year-Old Colt or Gelding of the Year. And in 2015, LC Zell and her junior rider finished the Tevis Cup in seventeenth place, the first completion of this historic ride for both of them.

Clearly, Orzel passed on his prodigious talent to many of his offspring, which in turn have handed it down to their descendants. The appearance of Orzel's name in a pedigree, even many generations removed, continues to have value to knowledgeable breeders. As artist and writer C.W. Anderson noted, "A great sire is not always a great racehorse, and conversely a great racehorse does not always prove to be a great sire. But when you see a great champion of the track duplicate his performances as a sire, you can rest assured that there was truly greatness in him. A single star may come from nowhere, but when others follow, that is no accident. That is heredity."[139]

Chapter 7

A SPLENDID VITALITY

In October 1976, the same year Orzel won his last major championship, eighty-three-year-old Ed Tweed decided that it was time to retire from Arabian breeding. He had been facing health challenges for quite a while, and the loss of Skorage the previous year had been a big blow. In addition, Arabian showing and breeding had morphed into a full-blown industry, a multimillion-dollar business that Tweed wanted no part of. Scottsdale, too, had grown and changed substantially since Ed and Ruth had first visited it in the 1940s.

After offering his granddaughter Shelley Groom Trevor a dozen horses of her choice, Tweed planned to sell the majority of his herd, the result of twenty-five years' effort. He reached out first to "those who already own Brusally Arabians or have expressed an interest in doing so…In this way, perhaps your hopes and dreams may merge with mine, and my retirement may be brightened by the knowledge that the Brusally bloodlines are in good hands and will continue to represent the finest in Arabian breeding."[140] Except for a few horses he wished to keep for sentimental reasons, including a son of Skorage, Tweed's herd was dispersed to like-minded Arabian breeders.

The next year, Tweed suffered a stroke. Trevor and Nancy Reidhead, an employee whom Tweed called his "right-hand woman," recalled, "Doctors had little hope for his survival, but they hadn't counted on the indomitable spirit of this grand old man. When he regained consciousness and found that he was partially paralyzed, Ed asked for pencil and paper. With his good hand, he drew plans for an apparatus that would move him from his

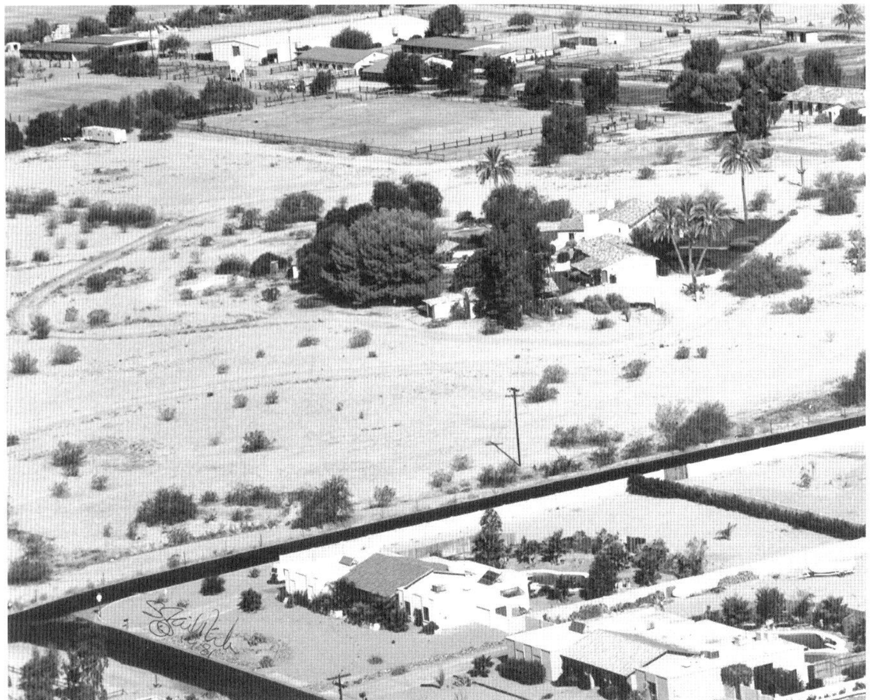

A 1981 photograph showing how much development had occurred around Brusally Ranch since the 1940s. *Photo by S. Gail Miller, courtesy of Shelley Groom Trevor.*

bed at home to a favorite chair"—and then he asked a trusted friend to execute the design. Although his movement was curtailed, his pleasure in interacting with others was not. He entertained visitors, dictated hundreds of letters and recorded messages on reel-to-reel tapes that were sent to friends worldwide. "Visitors seemed to sense the harmony and serenity [at Brusally], as though the inspiration of beauty and integrity were contagious."[141] Tweed lived for six years after his stroke and died at home on June 27, 1983, three weeks shy of his ninetieth birthday. Reidhead's condolence letter to Trevor read, in part:

> *I know and appreciate something of what he meant to you, something of what you meant to him—how deep the tie. And I want to celebrate the true greatness of the man—a spirit that never died, a dignity that remained intact, a courtliness that persevered, a humor that transcended pain—a sense of life and beauty and joy that nurtured a splendid vitality for nearly 90 years. Be proud that his blood runs in your veins as you fly over the hurdles.[142]*

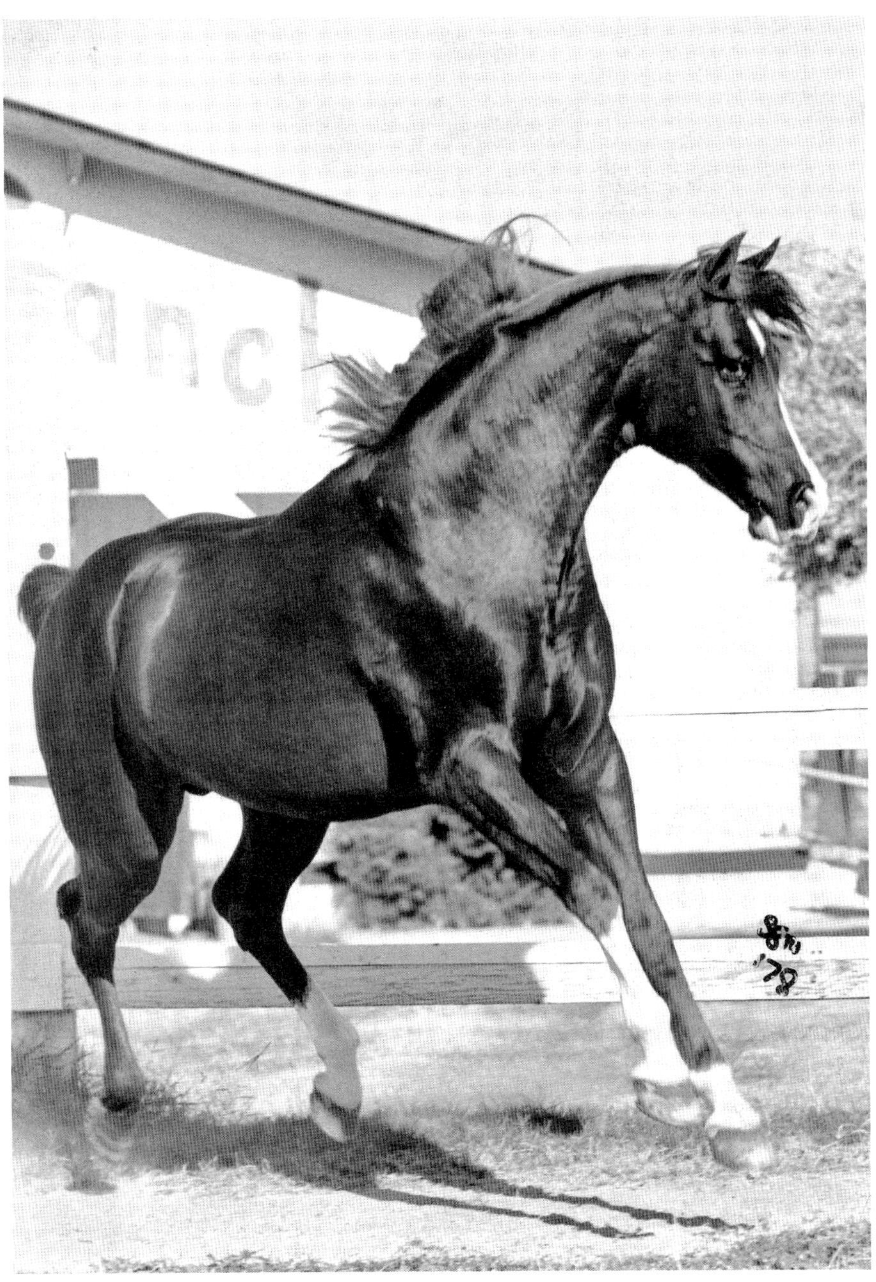

Orzel—a "triple threat" in racing, halter and performance—has thousands of descendants worldwide, performing at the highest level of their respective sports. *Photo by S. Gail Miller, courtesy of Shelley Groom Trevor.*

Tweed's most important legacies in the Arabian horse community are the Scottsdale Arabian Horse Show, which he cofounded; the Arizona Arabian Horse Association, for which he served as a founding member and its first president; and, of course, his breeding program, which produced nearly four hundred horses. Three of his equines have been elected to the Arabian Horse Trust's Racing Hall of Fame for their contributions to the sport: Orzel in 1995 and the stellar Polish broodmares Chlosta and Genua in 2000. At the 2006 Scottsdale Show, Tweed was posthumously inducted into the Arabian Horse Trust's Racing Tent of Honor, which lauded his "character, significant impact and dedication to Arabian breeding."[143] His daughter Sally Tweed Groom and granddaughter Shelley Groom Trevor accepted the honor on his behalf.

Orzel, understandably, had been the first horse that Trevor chose for herself from her grandfather's herd, and she looked forward to sharing many years with "her horse of a lifetime," as well as the others she had selected, including her dressage mounts Brusally Orzetyn and Brusally Orzelyna. However, soon after Tweed passed away, Orzel became gravely ill. Trevor shipped him to the family's ranch in the pines near Show Low, Arizona, where he could escape the desert heat and be cared for by ranch managers Nancy Reidhead and Bob Stanley. A little over a year after

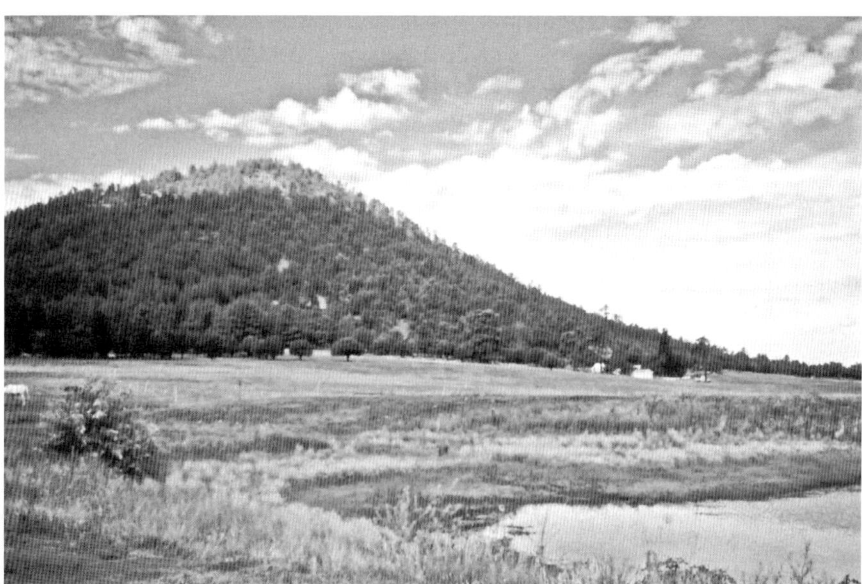

Ziegler Mountain overlooks the Tweeds' ranch in Show Low, Arizona, 2010. *Photo by and courtesy of the author.*

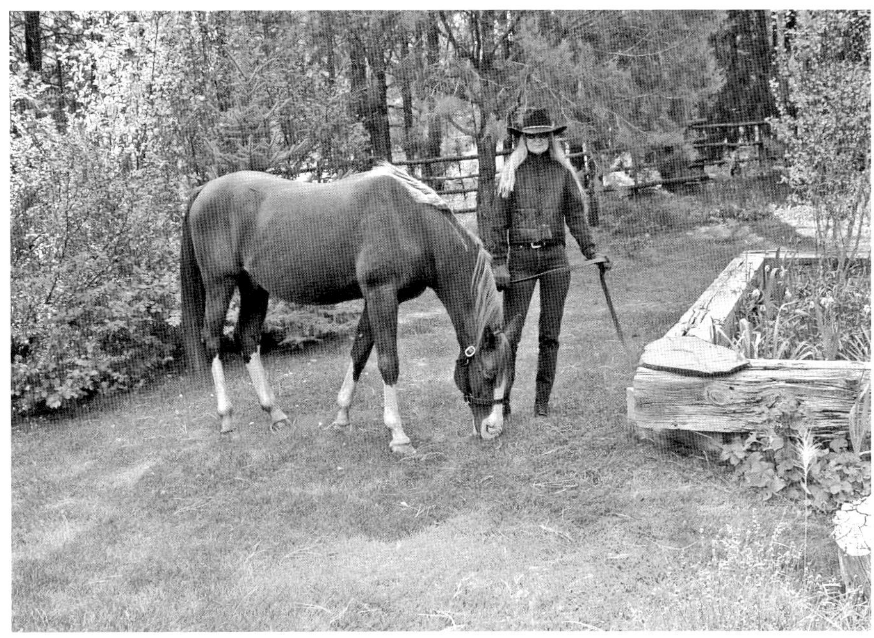

Champion LA Orzel, held by Trevor, grazes near the grave of his famous grandsire in 2007. *Photo by Richard Loveless, courtesy of the author.*

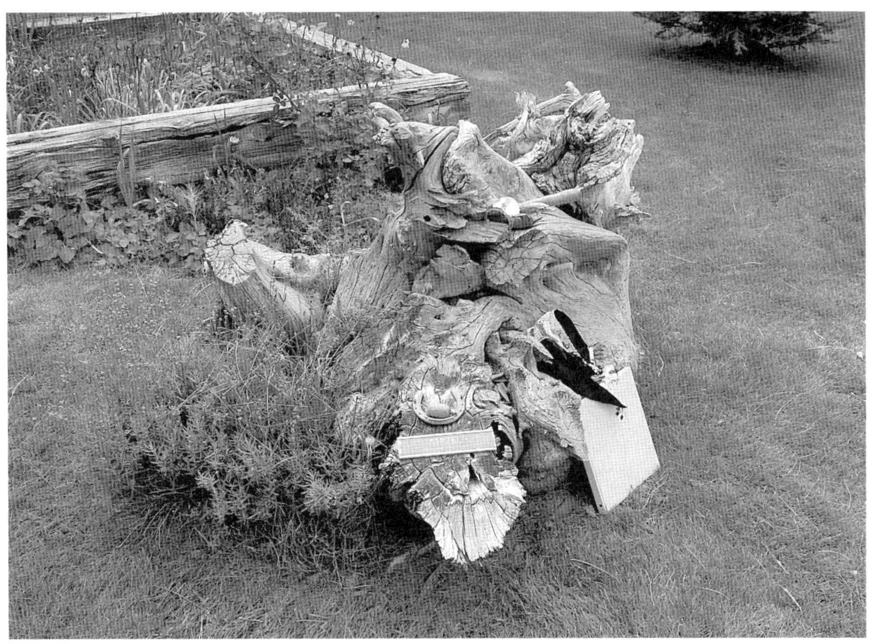

The grave of Tweed's champion in Orzel Park. *Photo by Richard Loveless, courtesy of the author.*

Tweed passed away, Orzel died on August 29, 1984. Coincidentally, this was the same day that Tweed's heirs sold the majority of his Scottsdale ranch to developers.[144]

Ziegler Mountain, at about 7,700 feet, provides a dramatic backdrop to the Tweed family's remaining ranch in the White Mountains. Although other Brusally horses had been buried on the edges of the ranch property over the years, Reidhead and Stanley felt that Orzel merited a permanent memorial, Orzel Park, in a picturesque spot. They selected a lush clearing, partially ringed by trees, near the foot of Ziegler Mountain. Once Orzel's massive body was finally interred in the grave they had so laboriously dug, the two "watched in amazement, disbelief, and with tears in their eyes as an eagle, for which Orzel was named, rose from that very spot, flying upward toward the mountain."[145] Orzel's spirit had at last taken its leave.

Today, Trevor has a small ranch north of Scottsdale, where she rides and trains her Brusally horses, all of them descendants of Orzel. Also a professional painter, she finds much inspiration for her works by simply being with her beloved equines. She particularly treasures the deep connection she's forged with her two chestnuts, LA Orzel and Brusally Flamenco, both of them the living legacy of the flame-colored stallion that carried her beyond her greatest dreams.[146]

ORZEL'S PEDIGREE

Sire: Pietuszok	Priboj	Piolun	Koheilan I
			Dziewanna
		Rissalma	Shareer
			Rissla
	Taktika	Taki Pan	Kaszmir
			Dziwa
		Krona	Kann
			Star of the Hills
Dam: Ofirka	Ofir	Kuhailan Haifi	Desert Bred
			Desert Bred
		Dziwa	Abu Mlech
			Zulejma
	Fryga II	Bakszysz	Ilderim
			Parada
		Gazella II	Kohejlan
			Abra

ORZEL'S RACE RECORD AND RACING AWARDS

OFFICIAL RACES IN POLAND

DATE	PLACING	DISTANCE	TIME	NOTES
Jul. 7, 1966	1	1,600m	1:58	
Aug. 10, 1966	n/a	1,800m	2:13	Race annulled for being excessively slow
Aug. 21, 1966	2	1,800m	2:07	
Sept. 4, 1966	3	1,800m	2:08	
Sept. 18, 1966	1	1,800m	2:10	
Oct. 16, 1966	2	2,400m	2:55	Criterium Stakes
Oct. 30, 1966	2	2,200m	2:43	Amurath Stakes

OFFICIAL PARIMUTUEL RACES IN THE UNITED STATES

DATE	PLACING	DISTANCE	TIME	WEIGHT
Sept. 4, 1967	1	1 mile, 4½ furlongs	3:04 4/5	116
Sept. 9, 1967	1	1 mile, 4½ furlongs	3:00 3/5	118
Nov. 19, 1967	2	1½ miles	2:49 1/5	130
Feb. 25, 1968	1	1½ miles	2:51 4/5	140
Mar. 30, 1968	1	1½ miles	2:49 4/5	142

COMBINED OFFICIAL RACE RECORD

YEAR	STARTS	FIRST	SECOND	THIRD	ANNULLED
1966	7	2	3	1	1
1967	3	2	1		
1968	2	2			
Total	12	6	4	1	1

RACING AWARDS

1967 U.S. National Champion Racehorse
1995 Inductee, Arabian Horse Trust Racing Hall of Fame

ORZEL'S MAJOR SHOW RING ACCOMPLISHMENTS

1969 Champion stallion, Las Vegas Arabian Horse Association

1969 Champion stallion, Arabian Horse Association of Southern California, Santa Barbara

1969 U.S. National Top Ten Stallion, Oklahoma City

1970 Champion stallion, Scottsdale Arabian Horse Show

1970 Champion stallion, Kansas All Arabian Show, Salina

1970 Champion stallion, Texas Arabian Horse Show, Dallas

1971 Champion stallion, Golden Spike All Arabian Horse Show, Ogden, Utah

1971 Region 5 Top Five Stallion, State Fair of Texas, Dallas

1971 Canadian National Top Ten Stallion, Edmonton, Alberta

1972 Champion stallion, Comstock All Arabian Horse Show, Reno

1972 English pleasure champion, Comstock All Arabian Horse Show, Reno

1972 Champion stallion, Las Vegas Arabian Horse Association Show

1972 Pacific Slope English pleasure champion, Grand National Horse Show, San Francisco

1972 Proud Performer, U.S. National Championships

1973 English pleasure champion, Oklahoma Arabian Horse Club Show, Oklahoma City

1973 English pleasure champion, North Texas All Arabian Horse Show, Dallas

1973 Region 1 Top Five English Pleasure, Sierra Empire All Arabian Show, Pomona, California

1973 U.S. National Top Ten English Pleasure, Oklahoma City

1973 Legion of Merit given at Scottsdale Arabian Horse Show

1974 U.S. National Champion Ladies' Sidesaddle, Albuquerque

1976 Ladies' sidesaddle champion, International Arabian Horse Fair, Reno, Nevada

ORZEL'S REGISTERED PUREBRED ARABIAN PROGENY

Key

G= gelding
M= mare
S = stallion
B = bay
C = chestnut
Gr = gray

APPENDIX D

NAME	YEAR OF BIRTH	SEX	COLOR	DAM	DAM'S SIRE	PERFORMANCE WINS
EW Gwee-zel	1969	G	C	El Wicu Naja	Alli-Moor	Regional Top Five Stock
Brusally Oraba	1969	M	C	Abhazja	Faher	
Brusally Orzelyna	1969	M	Gr	Gontyna	Doktryner	U.S. National Top Ten Western Pleasure twice
Brusally Orzeluba	1970	M	B	Miroluba	Faher	
Brusally Orzelawa	1970	M	C	Bulawa	Laur	Western pleasure champion
Brusally-Orzelyn	1970	S	Gr	Gontyna	Faher	Western pleasure winner
Brusally Orzelost	1970	S	Gr	Chlosta	Faher	
Brusally Orzelisa	1971	M	B	Wislica	Branibor	
Mohawk Chief	1971	S	C	Easter Basket	Bask	U.S. National Top Ten Ladies' Sidesaddle
Taki	1971	G	C	Ghalii Sharima	Ghalii	
Brusally Ormiro	1971	M	Gr	Miroluba	Faher	
Brusally Orzetyn	1971	S	C	Gontyna	Doktryner	U.S. National Champion Third Level Dressage
Wayward Wind	1971	S	C	Bahazaa	Bahade	
Brusally Orlin	1972	G	B	Salinaa	Comet	Eventing winner

NAME	YEAR OF BIRTH	SEX	COLOR	DAM	DAM'S SIRE	PERFORMANCE WINS
Brusally Orstar	1972	S	B	Star of Erka	Al Marah Erka	Halter reserve champion
Brusally Orenka	1972	M	B	Daszenka	Trypolis	
Brusally Orzelsta	1972	M	C	Chlosta	Faher	
Arazel	1972	G	B	Aaraffa	Aarief	U.S. National Champion Futurity Gelding and three times U.S. National Top Ten Gelding
Brusally Orzelta	1972	M	C	Skoretta	Skorage	Canadian Reserve National Champion Stock and twice US National Top Ten Stock
Brusally Orzelon	1972	G	Gr	Gontyna	Doktryner	
Brusally Orzelaw	1972	S	C	Bulawa	Laur	Race winner
Staleys Orzella	1973	M	C	Brusally Skorenua	Skorage	
Lady Luck	1973	M	B	Nawojka	Wielki Szlem	Scottsdale Top Ten English pleasure
Brusally Orsalin	1973	S	B	Salinaa	Comet	
Star of Orzel	1973	M	B	Star of Erka	Al Marah Erka	English pleasure winner
Brusally Oranna	1973	M	Gr	Manna	Naborr	
Orzenifa	1973	M	C	Brusally Faronifa	Faraon	

APPENDIX D

NAME	YEAR OF BIRTH	SEX	COLOR	DAM	DAM'S SIRE	PERFORMANCE WINS
Brusally Orsta	1973	M	B	Chlosta	Faher	
Sharif Ibn Orzel	1973	S	Gr	Brusally Farifata	Faraon	
Ormir	1973	S	B	Miroluba	Faher	Race winner and Race Colt of the Year
Brusally Orin	1973	G	Gr	Algorina	Ali Said	4 U.S. and 3 Canadian National Top Ten Hunter titles
Star Orzel	1973	M	Gr	Sloopy	Ibn Fadjur	
Jarzel	1974	S	B	Jahrah	Seahorse Rocket	Western pleasure champion
Bry-Her Orzeltahl	1974	S	C	Brusally Faratahl	Faraon	
Brusally Orzelark	1974	G	C	Brusally Farka	Faraon	
BR Oreo	1974	S	C	Bint Zarifa	Zarife	
Fairyzel	1974	M	C	ML Magic-Fairy	Touch of Magic	
Bayora	1975	G	Gr	Jahrah	Seahorse Rocket	
Summer	1975	M	Gr	Sloopy	Ibn Fadjur	
Farazel	1975	M	C	Brusally Faronifa	Faraon	

NAME	YEAR OF BIRTH	SEX	COLOR	DAM	DAM'S SIRE	PERFORMANCE WINS
Jorzel	1975	M	C	Jordana	Justin	
Brusaly[sic] Orzelosta	1976	M	Gr	Chlosta	Faher	
Scherzando	1976	S	C	Roczan	Seahorse Rocket	
Kona Queen	1976	M	C	Speed Queen	Ferana	Western pleasure champion
Orzelon	1976	G	B	Sloopy	Ibn Fadjur	
Royal Orzel	1976	G	C	Royal Kitten	Buck Ferseyn	English pleasure champion
Magus	1976	S	C	ML Magic Fairy	Touch of Magic	
Tamor-Zel	1976	G	C	Tamashar	Na Almaz	Regional Champion Western Pleasure and 3 other Regional titles
Bint Storama	1976	M	C	Storama	Gastorm	
Cassels Orzel	1976	S	Gr	Brusally Czina	Czester	
Brusally Orselar	1976	S	B	Cerera	Ferrum	
Shahona Queen	1977	M	C	Speed Queen	Ferana	
Babe	1977	M	B	Miroluba	Faher	

APPENDIX D

NAME	YEAR OF BIRTH	SEX	COLOR	DAM	DAM'S SIRE	PERFORMANCE WINS
Brusally Orzelos	1977	G	B	Chlosta	Faher	
DW Orzefar	1977	G	C	Brusally Farazara	Faraon	Reining champion
Orzan	1977	M	C	Brusally Zbruella	Zbrucz	English pleasure winner
Dosca	1977	M	C	Socal Ardis	Ardahan	
Otiki	1977	M	C	Tikis Starletta	Kontiki	Race winner
Brusally Orlyna	1977	M	B	Brusally Orzelyna	Orzel	
BR Gay Contessa	1978	M	B	Brusaly-Brusalyna	Zbrucz	
Vallejo Orzella	1978	M	Gr	Regiseyna	Regis	
Whiteagle	1978	S	Gr	Brusally Farla	Faraon	
Cerazel	1978	G	B	Cerera	Ferrum	Western pleasure reserve champion
Brusally Orzelast	1978	S	C	Brusally Zbrusta	Zbrucz	Race winner
Brusally Oryna	1979	M	Gr	Brusally Zbruyna	Zbrucz	

NAME	YEAR OF BIRTH	SEX	COLOR	DAM	DAM'S SIRE	PERFORMANCE WINS
Orzels Zbrusalyna	1979	M	B	Brusaly-Brusalyna	Zbrucz	
Mabrys Othello	1979	S	B	Brusally Zbruabe	Zbrucz	
YAS Orzel	1980	G	C	Yasmin Kimmar	Ramaraas of Delta C	
Orzali	1980	M	C	Aljabalah	Abs Fancy	
Dividens Orzelita	1980	M	C	Brusally Zbruata	Zbrucz	
Brusally Oryn	1980	S	B	Brusally Zbruyna	Zbrucz	
Brusally Orlen	1980	S	C	Brusally Czlena	Brusally Czesta	Stakes winner
SMR Ibn Orzel	1981	S	Gr	Chlosta	Faher	Race winner
Brusally Orzaborr	1981	S	Gr	Brusally Naborrla	Naborr	Western pleasure reserve champion
Orzela	1981	M	C	Fagai	El Cap Fargo	Stakes winner
Brusally Zelyna	1981	M	C	Brusally Zbruyna	Zbrucz	Race winner and Race Mare of the Year

NAME	YEAR OF BIRTH	SEX	COLOR	DAM	DAM'S SIRE	PERFORMANCE WINS
SGR Valentina	1982	M	B	Brusally Zbrenua	Zbrucz	
Brusally Orsata	1982	M	B	Brusally Zbrusata	Zbrucz	
FMR Jankes	1982	S	C	Brusally Chlosta	Zbrucz	
Brusally Gazella	1982	M	Gr	Brusally Zbruyna	Zbrucz	
Dorzella	1983	M	C	BH Desert Rose	Al Kaher	
Brusally Gaysar	1983	S	B	Brusally Zbrusata	Zbrucz	Stakes winner
FMR Betania	1983	M	C	Brusally Basta	Zbrucz	
Gazella III	1983	M	Gr	BR Bint Chlosta	Zbrucz	
Dakshina	1983	M	B	Brusally Czlena	Brusally Czesta	
SGR Vayu	1983	S	B	Brusally Zbrenua	Zbrucz	Stakes winner
Basta-D	1983	M	B	Basta	Comet	

APPENDIX D

NAME	YEAR OF BIRTH	SEX	COLOR	DAM	DAM'S SIRE	PERFORMANCE WINS
FMR Kasia	1983	M	Gr	Brusally Zbruyna	Zbrucz	
FMR Grand Jubilee	1984	M	C	Genua	Grand	
Savorzel Steed	1984	S	C	Savvora	Ararose	
Orram	1984	S	C	Magna Terra Pizaz	Magna Terra Rajah	Race winner
Worzel	1984	G	Gr	Windrez	Indratez	Stakes winner
Ila	1984	M	C	Brusally Czlena	Brusally Czesta	Race winner
Orzel II	1984	S	C	TL Baskletta	Baskfire	Race winner
FMR Celebrate	1984	M	C	Brusally Zbruyna	Zbrucz	
Brusally Ofirka	1984	M	B	Brusally Genua	Zbrucz	
Orzels Keepsake	1984	M	B	Kismets Keepsake	Magnaterra Kismet	
Orzelro	1985	S	C	Razigero	Razztero	Endurance competitor

NOTES

INTRODUCTION

1. Shelley Trevor, "*Orzel++," *Arabian Finish Line* (January–February 1993): 12.

CHAPTER 1

2. Deb Bennett, "The Origin of Horse Breeds," *Equus*, April 2014, 60.

3. Ibid., "The Arabian Horse," *Equus*, June 2014, 61–62.

4. Olsen and Culbertson, *Gift from the Desert*, 75.

5. Landry, *Noble Brutes*, 94.

6. Daumas, *Horses of the Sahara*, 57.

7. Dodge in Conn, *Arabian Horse in Fact*, 77–78.

8. Edwards, *Ultimate Horse Book*, 38.

9. Von Velsen-Zerweck and Schulte, *Trakehner*, 6–7.

10. Daumas, *Horses of the Sahara*, 11.

11. Archer, *Arabian Horse*, 3.

12. Landry, *Noble Brutes*, 2, 91, 95.

13. Conn, *Arabian Horse in America*, 13.

14. Edwards, *The Arabian*, 29.

15. https://www.google.com/fusiontables/DataSource?dsrcid=225439#rows:id=1.

16 Charles Craver and Jeanne Craver, "Horses of the White City, Part I," *Arabian Horse World*, September 1989, 138.

17. Ibid.

18. Ibid.; Gulsen Sevinc and Ayse Fazlioglu, "Turkish Participation to [*sic*] 1893 Chicago Exposition," *Turkish Yearbook of International Relations*, 2000.

19. Craver and Craver, "Horses of the White City, Part I," 140–41.

20. Davenport, *My Quest of the Arab Horse*, 3–4.

21. William H. Lee, *Beautiful Scenes of the White City*, 1894.

22. A list of the auctioned horses and their buyers is provided in Mulder, *Imported Foundation Stock*, Vol. 1, 11.

23. Orzel's official American name, according to the Arabian Horse Registry, is *Orzel++, and his registry number is 41019. The asterisk preceding his name indicates that he was imported to the United States, and the ++ following his name means that he won the Legion of Merit, the particulars of which are discussed in Chapter 5. Except in quoted material, he is referred to in this book simply as Orzel. For ease of reading, I have elected to refer to other imported horses in this book without using the asterisk appended to their names by the registry.

CHAPTER 2

24. Paul Hunter, "Day by Day," *Wisconsin State Journal*, August 22, 1937, 5.

25. *Under the Fig Tree* (newsletter), "Rotary's First Act of Service," October 2007, 4.

26. Harris, *This Rotarian Age*, 18.

27. In the autumn of 2014, during the writing of this book, two photographs of a signed copy of Hemingway's *The Old Man and the Sea* were posted on the site Imgur.com. The book, which the original poster claimed had been purchased at a yard sale for "two bucks," was inscribed: "To Carleton and Suzanna Tweed with all best wishes always from their friend Ernest Hemingway" (http://imgur.com/a/Bp7Ae). It is unclear how the Tweeds made Hemingway's acquaintance, though presumably they met when they all resided in Florida.

28. Dixie Ryan, "A Tribute to Ed Tweed," *Arabian Horse News*, July 1975, 40.

29. *Kansas Citian*, "Bank Engineers Win High Favor," August 25, 1931, 13.

30. Ryan, "Tribute to Ed Tweed," 41.

31. Hunter, "Day by Day," 5.

32. Shelley Groom and Nancy Reidhead, "The Brusally Story," *Arabian Horse World*, January 1984, 887.

33. Coventry et al., *Classic Country Estates*, 27.

34. Ibid., 283.

35. *Chicago Tribune*, "Arizona Dude Ranches Have Home Comforts," January 24, 1943.

36. Judith Cass, "Arizona Desert Resort Beckons Chicago Vacationers," *Chicago Tribune*, November 12, 1946.

37. Merle B. Cheney obituary, *Scottsdale Daily Progress*, December 22, 1977.

38. Ryan, "Tribute to Ed Tweed," 41.

39. Parkinson, *And Ride Away Singing*.

40. Mary Jane Parkinson, "Anne McCormick," *Arabian Horse World*, December 1985.

41. VanderMeer and VanderMeer, *Phoenix Rising*, 12.

42. Ellinger, *Brusally Arabians*, 5–6.

43. Gladys Brown Edwards, "The Gainey Story," *Arabian Horse Journal*, April 1961.

44. Ryan, "Tribute to Ed Tweed," 41.

45. Ellinger, *Brusally Arabians*, 7–9.

46. Bob O'Shaughnessy, "Van Vleet's Arabian 'Laboratory,'" *Western Horseman*, March/April 1944.

47. Edwards, *The Arabian*, 80.

48. Covey, *Crabbet Arabians*, 34.

49. Varianarabians.com.

50. Parkinson, *And Ride Away Singing*, 30.

51. Jim Robbins, "The Selby Stud—Part 1," *Crabbet Influence in Arabians Today* (February/March 1995).

52. Carpenter, *Arabian Legends*, 200.

53. Ellinger, *Brusally Arabians*, 9.

54 Dickson Hartwell, "A Fine Horsewoman Becomes Leading Painting of Animal Portraits in Valley," *Arizonian*, February 20, 1964.

55. Carpenter, *Arabian Legends*, 197. It also should be noted that, although the Arabian Horse Registry's database (arabdatasource.com) lists sixty-nine purebred foals for Skorage, this total does not include two purebred foals that had to be registered as half-Arabians because of the registry's rules regarding Russian-bred Arabians at that time. These two foals, Brusally Skormira (born 1966) and Brusally Skoramir (born 1967), were out of Palmira, one of three Russian Arabians imported by Tweed in 1963. For more information, see the chapter on Palmira in Taylor, *Polish and Russian Arabians*, 2013.

56. Mary Jane Parkinson, "Prizes of War: Polish Imports, 1945," *Arabian Horse World*, June 1981.

57. Lipowicz and Zbyszewski, *Arabian Horse*, 25.

58. Schiele, *Arabian Horse in Europe*, 71–72.

CHAPTER 3

59. Emilie "Rainbow" Touraine interview, June 12, 2012.

60. Nicole Swengley, "Links in the Chain," *Evening Standard*, March 25, 2005.

61. Taylor, *Polish and Russian Arabians*.

62. Letter report to Ed Tweed from Brusally trainer Steve Spalding, April 21, 1963. Courtesy of Shelley Groom Trevor.

63. Ibid., April 2, 1963. Courtesy of Shelley Groom Trevor.

64. Shelley Groom Trevor, "Ed Tweed and Brusally Ranches: The Story of Arizona's Pioneer Arabian Horse Breeder," *Western Horseman*, April 1999, 99.

65. Ryan, "Tribute to Ed Tweed," 48.

66. Edwards, *Photographic History*, 114.

CHAPTER 4

67. Shelley Groom Trevor, "*Orzel++, Arabian Racing Superstar!" *Arabian Racing Illustrated*, July 1998, 38.

68. Gladys Brown Edwards, "Racing '69," *Arabian Horse World*, August 1969, 90.

69. Carolyn Gipson, "The *Orzel Son Magus," *Arabian Racing Illustrated*, July 1998, 62.

70. Gladys Brown Edwards, "Piolun," *Arabian Horse World*, November 1981, 187.

71. John Schiewe, February 11, 2010. http://forums.arabianbreeders.net/index.php?/topic/33875-foaling-season-in-poland/page-2.

72. Arlene Caverly, "*Pietuszok's Last Home," *Arabian Horse World*, June 1981; Cheryl G. Himes, "*Pietuszok," *Arabian Visions*, November, 1989.

73. I thank Andra Kowalczyk Martens for providing information on two race winners, Barbados and Le Bajram, as well as one nonwinner, El Wicu Facia.

74. Himes, "*Pietuszok," 21.

75. Lipowicz and Zbyszewski, *Arabian Horse*, 115.

76. Ibid., 116.

77. Schiele, *Arabian Horse in Europe*, 166.

78. Lipowicz and Zbyszewski, *Arabian Horse*, 117.

79. R.J. Cadranell, "Janow Podlaski Between the Wars: A Road Map for Beginners," *Arabian Visions*, February 1990, 102.

80. Lipowicz and Zbyszewski, *Arabian Horse*, 117.

81. Schiele, *Arabian Horse in Europe*, 168.

82. Lipowicz and Zbyszewski, *Arabian Horse*, 81.

83. Ibid., 111.

84. Pankiewicz, *Seven Splendids.*

85. Lipowicz and Zbyszewski, *Arabian Horse*, 110.

86. Harriette Spencer, "The Influence of Ofir in America," *Arabian Horse News*, February 1972, 55.

87. Gladys Brown Edwards, "Ofir," *Arabian Horse World*, November 1981, 198.

88. Pankiewicz, *Breeding of Pure Blood Arabian*, 12.

89. Ibid., 12–13.

90. Skorkowski, *Arab Breeding in Poland*, 37.

91. Rozwadowski, *50 Years of Breeding Pure Blood Arabian Horses*, 10.

92. Jakub Kasprzak, Polish Jockey Club, e-mails of August 21 and 22, 2015.

93. Gladys Brown Edwards, "Racing Time…and Times," *Arabian Horse World*, December 1967, 46.

94. It is possible that Edwards, who apparently had her own Polish-language copy of Orzel's record, may not have known the meaning of the Polish phrase *gonitwa uniewazniona* (race annulled) on the chart for his second race and thus (sometimes) counted Orzel's third-place finish in this annulled race among his *valid* starts. In two 1960s-era articles for *Arabian Horse World*, as well as information she provided to breeder Joe Cassel, Edwards listed seven starts, including Orzel's (invalid) third-place finish (i.e., 1/7[2-3-2]), whereas in a 1975 article and two 1980s-era publications, she listed seven total starts and only one third-place finish (i.e., 1/7[2-3-1]). In none of these articles did she mention that one of Orzel's races was invalid, nor did she apparently convey that information to Cassel, suggesting that she was unaware of that fact. See Edwards, "Racing Resume," *Arabian Horse World*, July 1968, 76; Edwards, "Racing '69," 90; Edwards, "The Record Speaks," *Arabian Horse World*, September 1975, 234; Edwards, *Photographic History*, 111; Edwards, "Race Stallions: A Few from the Winner's Circle," *Arabian Horse World*, August 1988, 317. Cassel discusses receiving Orzel's Polish race record from Edwards in his article "The Life and Times of *Orzel," *Arabian Racing Illustrated*, July 1998, 56.

95. Edwards, "Race Stallions," 317.

96. Ibid., 317.

97. Trevor, "Orzel++, Arabian Racing Superstar!" 38.

98. Edwin J. Tweed, letter to Edward Skorkowski of September 6, 1968. Copy in possession of Shelley Groom Trevor.

99. Don Thiel, "National Show Racing at Albuquerque, New Mexico, August 11–13, 1967," *Arabian Horse World*, October 1967, 128–31.

100. Trevor, "*Orzel++, Arabian Racing Superstar!" 40.

101. Kowalczyk, *Tennessee's Arabian Horse Racing Heritage*, 55.

102. *Arizona Republic*, "Turf Charts," November 20, 1967.

103. A number of writers, myself included, have uncritically repeated versions of Edwards's erroneous statement that "Orzel was bested by El Gohari but beat him in their second encounter" when, in fact, it was El Gohari that bested Orzel in their second encounter; Edwards, "Record Speaks," 234; Edwards, "Race Stallions," 317; Taylor, *Polish and Russian Arabians*, 124; Sarah A. Wax, "Green Pastures," *Arabian Horse World*, January 1985, 292.

104. *Arabian Horse World*, "World News: First Phoenix Race a Crowd-Pleaser; Sixty Arabian in Training at Arizona Track," December 1967, 80.

105. *Arizona Republic*, "Arizona Downs," February 26, 1968.

106. Ibid., "Yesterday's Arizona Downs Results," March 31, 1968.

107. Edwards, "Racing Resume," 71.

CHAPTER 5

108. Mary Jane Parkinson, "Foundation Breeder: The Tweed Family, Brusally Ranch," *Arabian Horse World*, February 2000, 157.

109. Ibid., 157–58.

110. Buff Ross, "Odes to the Lowcountry: Pluff Mud," Charlestonmag.com, http//:charlestonmag.com/features/pluff_mud.

111. Shelley Groom Trevor, "Women and Horses," *Arizona Horse Connection*, September 1988.

112. Carpenter, *Arabian Legends*, 200–01.

113. Shelley Groom Trevor, "A Riding Life," *Arizona Horse Connection*, April 2015.

114. Shirley H. Chartrand, "Highlights of Arizona," *National Horseman*, July 1968.

115. Shelley Groom Trevor, "Insights of Horsemanship—The Allure of the Horse," *Arizona Horse Connection*, February 1988.

116. Cheryl Rexford, "Horsemanship, Gamesmanship," *Arizona Republic*, September 9, 1968.

117. Shelley Groom Trevor, e-mail to author, June 25, 2015.

118. Ibid., July 15, 2015.

119. Trevor, "*Orzel++," 10.

120. Trevor, "*Orzel++, Arabian Racing Superstar!" 42.

121. Trevor, "*Orzel++," 12.

122. Letter to Ed Tweed from Walter Farley, August 29, 1974. In possession of Shelley Groom Trevor.

123. Ibid.

124. Walter Farley, "Letters from Walter Farley, Author of the 'Black Stallion' Series," *Arabian Horse World*, August 1970, 142.

125. Farley, letter to Tweed, August 29, 1974.

126. Shelley Groom Trevor, "*ORZEL+ (Pietuszok x Ofirka)," unpublished manuscript in possession of Trevor.

127. Cassel, "Life and Times of *Orzel," 58.

128. Clay interview, April 14, 2009.

CHAPTER 6

129. Shelley Groom, "Dressage World: Brusally Orzetyn (*Orzel x *Gontyna)," *Arabian Horse World*, June 1981, 64.

130. Ibid., 64, 579.

131. Ibid., 579.

132. *Arabian Horse World*, "Arazel+: Arabian Horse World's Four-Star Gelding Club No. 38," May 1979, 207.

133. Clay interview, 2009; advertisement, Kit Hall Arabians, *Arabian Horse World*, February 1978, 94.

134. Trevor, interview, August 1, 2012.

135. Gipson, "*Orzel Son Magus," 61.

136. Sired by a chestnut (Orzel) and out of a gray (Brusally Orzelyna), Brusally Orlyna was a bay mare with a great deal of white and sported a blue eye—the only blue eye among Orzel's offspring, as far as I am aware.

137. Gipson, "*Orzel Son Magus," 62–63.

138. In the text of my 2013 book, I erroneously listed the number of Orzel's total purebred foals as ninety-nine, not ninety-eight (though the total is correct in the book's appendix); see Taylor, *Polish and Russian Arabians*, 125. Records for Orzel's part-bred foals are scant. His three known part-bred foals are the half-Arabian gelding Aasif Ibn Orzel (Reg. No. A112811), which won the English pleasure amateur owner championship at the 1978 Silver Clover Show in Scottsdale; the half-Arabian mare Bint K-Chu (Reg. No. A107851), which qualified to compete in the stock horse championship at the 1977 U.S. National Championship show; and the Anglo-Arabian gelding A-Pageants Orzel (Reg. No. AA4726), which competed in one endurance ride in 1988.

139. Anderson, *Smashers*, 20.

CHAPTER 7

140. Sue Hesse, "The Column," *Arabian Horse World*, January 1977, 841.

141. Groom and Reidhead, "Brusally Story," 1,028.

142. Trevor, "Ed Tweed and Brusally Ranches," 99.

143. Stephanie Corum, "Racing Tent of Honor: Edwin J. Tweed," *Arabian Finish Line*, February 2006, 10.

144. Ed Tweed's Spanish Colonial–style home and some acreage surrounding it are all that remain of his Scottsdale ranch. This property, which is no longer in the Tweed family's possession, is also the last significant remnant of the 1950s–80s Arabian horse breeding scene in the city. The other large ranches and show grounds from that era have been replaced by housing developments, shopping malls and an automobile dealership.

145. Trevor, "*Orzel++, Arabian Racing Superstar!" 44.

146. Trevor, letter to author, May 18, 2015.

SOURCES

Anderson, C.W. *The Smashers: Twenty-four Great Horses of Our Time.* New York: Harper and Brothers, 1952.

Arabian Finish Line

Arabian Horse News

Arabian Horse World

Arabian Racing Illustrated

Archer, Rosemary. *The Arabian Horse.* London: J.A. Allen and Company, 1992.

Arizona Republic

The Arizonian

Carpenter, Marian K. *Arabian Legends: Outstanding Arabian Stallions and Mares.* Colorado Springs, CO: Western Horseman, Inc., 1999.

Chicago Tribune

Conn, George H. *The Arabian Horse in America.* New York: A.S. Barnes and Company, 1957.

Coventry, Kim, Daniel Meyer and Arthur H. Miller. *Classic Country Estates of Lake Forest: Architecture and Landscape Design, 1856–1940.* New York: W.W. Norton and Company, 2003.

Covey, Cecil. *Crabbet Arabians.* Crawley, Sussex: self-published, 1982.

Daumas, General E. *The Horses of the Sahara.* Austin: University of Texas Press, 1968.

Davenport, Homer. *My Quest of the Arab Horse.* New York: B.W. Dodge and Company, 1909.

Dodge, Theodore A. "Riders of Many Lands." In *The Arabian Horse in Fact, Fantasy, and Fiction*, edited by George H. Conn, 71–78. New York: A.S. Barnes and Company, 1959.

Edwards, Elwyn Hartley. *The Ultimate Horse Book.* New York: Dorling Kindersley, Inc., 1991.

SOURCES

Edwards, Gladys Brown. *The Arabian: War Horse to Show Horse.* Covina, CA: Rich Publishing, 1973.

———. *A Photographic History of the Polish Arabian.* Rockville, MD: Arab Ink, 1978.

Ellinger, Ed. *Brusally Arabians* (brochure). Scottsdale, AZ: Brusally Ranch, ca. 1960.

Harris, Paul P. *This Rotarian Age.* Chicago: Rotary International, 1935.

Kowalczyk, Andra. *Tennessee's Arabian Horse Racing Heritage.* Charleston, SC: Arcadia Publishing, 2007.

Landry, Donna. *Noble Brutes: How Eastern Horses Transformed Western Culture.* Baltimore, MD: Johns Hopkins University Press, 2009.

Lee, William H. *Beautiful Scenes of the White City: A Portfolio of Original Copper-plate Half-tones of the World's Fair, Its Marvelous Architectural Groups, Statuary, Interiors, Lagoons and Vivid Scenes from the Famous Midway Plaisance.* Farewell ed. Chicago: Laird and Lee, 1894.

Lipowicz, Zenon, and George Zbyszewski. *The Arabian Horse: Poland's National Treasure.* Waseca, MN: Arabian Horse Times, Inc., 2007.

Mulder, Carol June Woodbridge. *Imported Foundation Stock of North American Arabian Horses.* Vol. 1. Aptos, CA: self-published, 1991.

National Horseman

Olsen, Sandra L., and Cynthia Culbertson. *A Gift from the Desert: The Art, History, and Culture of the Arabian Horse.* Lexington: International Museum of the Horse, Kentucky Horse Park, 2010.

Pankiewicz, Roman. *The Breeding of Pure Blood Arabian Horse in Poland in Their Genealogical Charts, 1975–1978.* Warsaw, Poland: Panstwowe Wydawnictwo Rolnicze, 1979.

———. *Seven Splendids.* Kampinos, Poland: Korfowe Arabians, 1996.

Parkinson, Mary Jane. *…And Ride Away Singing: The Breeding Philosophy of Bazy Tankersley and the History of Al-Marah Arabians.* Tucson, AZ: Al-Marah Arabians/Arabian Horse Owners Foundation, 1998.

Rozwadowski, Zdzislaw. *50 Years of Breeding Pure Blood Arabian Horses in Their Genealogical Charts, 1918–1968.* Warsaw, Poland: Panstwowe Wydawnictwo Rolnicze, 1972.

Schiele, Erika. *The Arabian Horse in Europe: History and Present Breeding of the Pure Arab.* London: George G. Harrap and Company, 1970.

Scottsdale Daily Progress

Skorkowski, Edward. *Arab Breeding in Poland.* Columbus, WI: Your Pony, 1969.

Taylor, Tobi Lopez. *The Polish and Russian Arabians of Ed Tweed's Brusally Ranch.* Tucson, AZ: Mare's Nest Books/Screenfold Press, 2013.

VanderMeer, Philip, and Mary VanderMeer. *Phoenix Rising: The Making of a Desert Metropolis.* Carlsbad, CA: Heritage Media Corporation, 2002.

Von Velsen-Zerweck, Eberhard, and Erhard Schulte. *The Trakehner.* London: J.A. Allen and Company, 1990.

INDEX

ABOUT THE AUTHOR

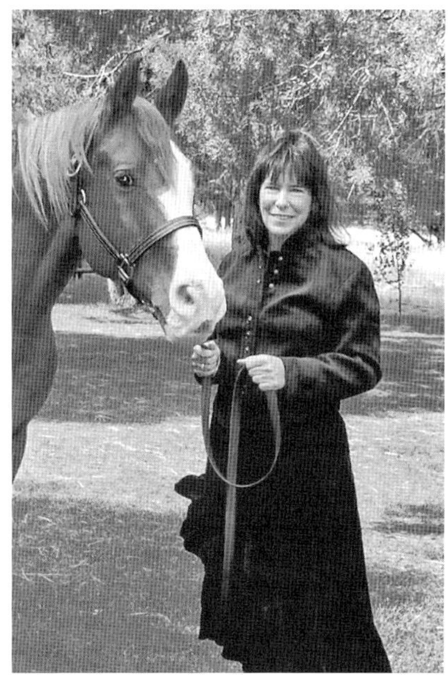

Tobi Lopez Taylor is an award-winning writer and editor. Trained as an anthropologist, she has bachelor's and master's degrees from Arizona State University. She is the author or co-author of two previous books, and her writing has been included in anthologies, as well as in various national magazines, including *American Indian Art Magazine*, *Archaeology Magazine*, *Blood-Horse*, *Dressage Today* and *Horse Illustrated*. Her first co-authored book won an Arizona Governor's Award in Historic Preservation, and an article she wrote on Arizona's Rillito Park Racetrack received a Sprint Award for excellence in equine journalism. She lives on a small ranch in southern Arizona, where she raises and rides Brusally Ranch–related Arabian horses, including descendants of Orzel.

Visit us at
www.historypress.net
....
This title is also available as an e-book